D0342957

WRITING IN AN
AGE OF SILENCE

WRITING IN AN AGE OF SILENCE

SARA PARETSKY

VERSO

London • New York

First published by Verso 2007

© Sara Paretsky 2007

This paperback edition published by Verso 2009

All rights reserved

1 3 5 7 9 10 8 6 4 2

Verso

UK: 6 Meard Street, London W1F 0EG

US: 20 Jay Street, Suite 1010, Brooklyn, NY 11201

www.versobooks.com

Verso is the imprint of New Left Books

ISBN-13: 978-1-84467-377-3

British Library Cataloguing in Publication Data

A catalogue record for this book is available from the British Library

Library of Congress Cataloging-in-Publication Data

A catalog record for this book is available from the Library of Congress

Typeset in Bodoni by Hewer Text UK Ltd, Edinburgh

Printed and bound by Maple Vail in the US

For Tom Phillips

Though much is taken, much abides; and though
We are not now that Strength which in old days
Moved Heaven and Earth, that which we are, we are
One equal temper of heroic hearts
Made weak by time and fate, but strong in will
Born to strive, to seek, to find, and not to yield

Tennyson, Ulysses

Contents

Introduction

One of my favorite books is *Caught in the Web of Words*, Elizabeth Murray's loving memoir of her grandfather, James A. H. Murray, who created the Oxford English Dictionary. I'd like to steal her title for a memoir of my own life. Among my earliest memories, besides proudly displaying a bleeding toe when I was three—proof in my mind that I belonged with the big children—or enraging my mother by washing off my first beloved pair of red shoes under the garden hose—are books, words, the smell of new books, which to me still heralds the excitement of the first day of school.

My older brother Jeremy taught me to read when he started school. I was about four, but I don't remember learning. I don't remember a time when I couldn't read. Jeremy was my first and always my best teacher, patient beyond belief (until the time came when I couldn't understand his explanation of fractions). He taught me to write, as well. When I was five and he was eight, we wrote plays that we put on for the other kids on our street.

I kept writing, all through my childhood and adolescence, stories, the occasional poem. Somehow I never wrote any other plays.

Jeremy and I read aloud to each other when we were teenagers. One summer we covered all of Shaw's plays; another time, we sang all of Gilbert & Sullivan to each other.

When Jeremy and I were responsible for washing all the dishes for our family of seven, we played word games or sang duets while we cleaned up. He's smarter than me and has always had a bigger vocabulary, so I started making up words to even the gap; he could never be certain whether to challenge me or not—if the word was in Webster's, I won, if not, he did. Creating uncertainty was my only weapon, and perhaps that sharpened my powers of invention.

My brother is a gifted linguist (he speaks eleven languages and reads fifteen); one year he added French lessons to the dishwashing hour. I used to look forward to washing up. After he left for college, the chore became just that, a dull chore. I hate it to this day.

While my older brother and I read together, my next brother, Dan, and I acted out dramas. Sometimes we emulated our three military uncles by acting out the Korean or Second World Wars; at other times we were Scotland Yard Detectives. My two youngest brothers, Jonathan and Nicholas, were so very much younger than I that we didn't often play together, but our time together was very important; I was to all intents their surrogate mother when our mother's life became too difficult for her to deal with and she withdrew into a private hell (when they started school, they didn't know I was their sister—they thought they had two mothers).

Before that time, our mother was an inventive story-teller. She had two long-running serials that she created for my younger brothers while she ironed. As a child, she had adored the Tom Mix movies, and she spun those into new versions, starring my brothers. I some-times eavesdropped, spellbound by her tales.

Perhaps it doesn't seem surprising that I became a writer, but it was, in fact, a difficult journey. This memoir traces the long path I followed from silence to speech, and the ways in which my speech has been shaped by what I've witnessed along the way. The book deals with the dominant question of my own life, the effort to find a voice, the effort to help others on the margins find a voice, the effort to understand and come to terms with questions of power and powerlessness. My husband says I am a pit dog, that I will go into the ring against anyone, as long as they are at least five times my size. I will turn sixty soon, but I still haven't figured out when it's time to walk away from a Goliath.

I have four brothers in all, three younger than I.[1] We had a childhood together that was rich in many aspects, but was also marred by the serious violence in our household. Like many violent families, we imploded on ourselves; it was hard for most of us to reach out and become connected to the larger world. My brothers are all interesting people, gifted in many ways, but it would be wrong of me to tell their stories for them, so as much as possible I have tried not to present anecdotes in which they were the key players.

I was born in Ames, Iowa, where my father was completing his PhD in bacteriology. He was a New Yorker, a City College man, but for a time in the thirties and forties, Iowa State College became home to some of the most gifted biochemists of the twentieth century as Jewish refugees from Hitler's Europe found a home there. My father's City College professors sent him to Iowa to study with these brilliant scientists. My mother had also gone to Iowa for graduate study; she and my father met there as students.

My father was drafted shortly after they married. He spent the Second World War in the Pacific theater; she worked for a short time in New York, living with his family, then spent the rest of the war years with her mother and her new baby, my brother Jeremy, in downstate Illinois. In 1951, my father took a position in the Bacteriology Department at the University of Kansas. My mother did not finish her advanced degree in science, nor did she work outside the home until much later in her life, when she became the children's librarian in Lawrence, Kansas.[2]

Harriet Martineau wrote of a southern politician that "he was born old." This is how I often feel on looking back on my childhood.[3] The first chapter in this collection, "Wild Women Out of Control," discusses that part of my life.[4]

When my parents decreed that I had to attend the

University of Kansas if I was going to go to university at all, I made a private vow that I would spend my summers away from home. The first year, I earned a scholarship to Vienna to study German; the second summer, in 1966, I went to Chicago to do community service work on the city's South Side.

The summer I spent in Chicago changed my life in almost every important way. I wasn't then imagining that I would be a writer, but the people I worked with and the work I did shaped the way in which I looked at the world around me. Those were turbulent times, but also times of great hopefulness among those who longed for social justice. Dr. Martin Luther King, Jr. was organizing in Chicago during the summer of 1966 and I was on the periphery of his great work. The way in which my experiences of that epoch became a major influence on my novels is the subject of the second chapter, "The King and I."

My father was a mercurial man, charming, nervous, but subject to rages that were all the more bewildering because we never knew what might trigger them. For the first twenty years of my life, he dominated almost every aspect of my existence. When I finally started university, he even decided what courses I would take. It took many years of many different kinds of support— from the man I later married, from psychotherapy, but above all, from the women's movement of the seventies—before I gained an independent voice. The third chapter explains the importance of Second Wave Fem-

inism in my life. It was feminism that triggered my
wish to write a private eye novel, and it shaped the
character of my detective, V I Warshawski.[5]

The private eye is America's unique contribution to
the crime novel. It comes out of our fascination with the
loner heroes of the old West. The fourth chapter, "The
iPod and Sam Spade," discusses the way in which
American mythology glorifies the individual often at
the expense of society. I also explore the ways in which
my own understanding of the individual and society
invert this mythology.

The town where I grew up in the fifties was obsessed by
the threat of Communism. Freedom committees, the
John Birch society, and other right-wing groups mon-
itored everything from school curricula to books in the
library; they ran a sideline in monitoring whether
African-Americans were using public facilities. They
forced the resignation of a high school teacher because
he was getting a PhD in Russian history—proof in their
eyes that he was a Communist.

The McCarthy hearings, which took place when I was
in primary school, left the adults in my life very cautious
in what they said politically, and who they said it to. My
parents had friends who were blacklisted; it's possible
that because my father had leftist relatives my mother's
military brothers were kept from being promoted.

Like all Americans, I am the descendant of immigrants. Some of my ancestors came here for adventure

or to make a better living, but most of them, on both sides of my family, came here to escape religious persecution. For my paternal grandparents, America meant the difference between life and death.

I grew up with a very idealized vision of what the country should be and could be. I grew up believing in the America of the Statue of Liberty. The Lady with the Lamp said to the world, "Give me your tired, your hungry, your poor/the wretched refuse of your teeming shores/send these, the weary, tempest-tossed to me/I lift my lamp beside the golden door."

When Congress passed the USA Patriot Act in the weeks following 9/11, the name of the act itself seemed to me to be Orwellian, the kind of title Stalin or Hitler or Franco might have chosen, one that tried to force people to choose sides. "You are either with us or against us," Mr. Bush famously told the world, but he was delivering the same message at home. "You're a patriot or a terrorist," the Patriot Act screams in its very title. Indeed, in the run-up to the now-famous elections of 2006, when the Republicans lost control of Congress, Mr. Bush toured the country, proclaiming that a vote for Democrats meant, "The terrorists win and America loses."[6]

Overnight, Congress and the President had created a law which undercut our most cherished liberties, including the right to be free from unreasonable search and seizure. In the five years since the Act was passed, we citizens have been given no credible examples of its use in stopping terrorism, but it has been extensively used to curtail civil liberties at home.

I am writing this in the late fall of 2006. I can't possibly predict the direction the new Congress will take in redressing some of these issues, but I am troubled by their unwillingness to revisit the Military Comissions Act, or the Patriot Act, which was both reauthorized and broadened by the outgoing Congress.

I began speaking on the topic of speech and silence to state library associations in 2002, since libraries were on the frontline of some of the Act's most pernicious sections. In May, 2004, *Booklist*, one of the journals of the American Library Association, published a portion of my lecture. The title, "Truth, Lies and Duct-Tape," comes from the administration's witty advice to a nation terrified of biological warfare: we were told to seal up our houses with duct tape, which caused a run on the stuff, and at least had the benefit of driving up the manufacturer's per-share price. The fifth chapter in this collection is a substantially rewritten, updated version of that essay. The middle three chapters, "The King and I," "Not Angel, Not Monster, Just Human," and "The iPod and Sam Spade," have never been published. In the course of any year, I deliver about six to ten public speeches. Portions of all five chapters have been used in some of my lectures. People who have attended have often asked for written copies of them—here they are, expanded, rewritten, updated.

Because this memoir is short, focusing on questions

of voice and voicelessness, I couldn't find an appropriate way to write about a number of people and events of great importance to me. Above all, my husband, Courtenay Wright, deserves a book of his own (indeed, he is very worried about my efforts to write his autobiography). He is a man of humor, a brilliant particle physicist, a former radar signal officer in the Royal Navy (General Eisenhower used my husband's ship, the *HMS Apollo*, as his headquarters when he sailed to Normandy on D-Day plus 1. My husband was the serving officer on the bridge when the ship went aground. As the most junior man present, he wisely—and uncharacteristically—kept his mouth shut, but the General's startled face was inches from his own as the ship pitched to one side). Above all, my husband is a man of great integrity. I have never known his equal.

Notes

1 For the interested reader, my older brother became a Dominican priest. He taught in Rome for many years but currently works in New York. Daniel, two years younger than I, is a veterinarian in northern Wisconsin. Jonathan, nine years younger, is a Kansas lawyer, a magician, an astronomer. He and Nicholas, the youngest, used to play table tennis together in a room in our basement that had once been a hiding place on the Underground Railroad. Nicholas recently completed a PhD in sociology, with a brilliant, beautifully written thesis on the way in which multi-nationals affect government economic policy.

2 Her dedication to books and children's literacy led the library to name the children's reading room for her. The day of her funeral, they had to close the library, since all of her co-workers needed to say farewell to her.

3 Martineau was writing of South Carolina senator John C. Calhoun, who was the south's leading apologist for slavery. It's the image of my own life, not the subject of his work, that I find applicable. Calhoun rightly pointed out the economic benefits the north reaped from slavery, which made them reluctant to seek its overthrow.

4 A portion of "Wild Women Out of Control" was published in *Family Portraits*, Doubleday & Col, 1985.

5 First Wave Feminism is usually thought to have started with the Seneca Falls Convention of 1848, in which women first formally came together to demand suffrage and an end to their legal and economic subjugation, and ended with the 19th Amendment to the US Constitution, which granted women suffrage in 1920. Second Wave Feminism doesn't have such a definable beginning point. Just as First Wave Feminism grew out of women's involvement in Abolition, the Second Wave grew out of women's involvement in the Civil Rights movement.

6 Cited, *inter alia*, in the *Washington Post*, October 31, 2006.

1

Wild Women Out of Control,
or How I Became a Writer

At four the little girl's hair is a frizzy mass, a knot of
tight curls around her head instead of the fine
straight silk of other girls her age. Her mother makes a
forlorn attempt to set it right, to put it in pin curls and
smooth it out. But when the bobby pins come off,
instead of the glossy curls the mother hoped for, the
daughter's frizz now stands up wildly all over her head.

"Witch! You're a witch!" Her older brother dances in a
circle around her, pointing and doubling up in laughter.

The little girl scowls. "I *am* a witch," she says
menacingly. "And witches know everything."

The brother's laughter collapses. He races to the
kitchen calling to his mother. "Sara says she's a witch
and witches know everything. She doesn't really know
everything, does she?"

Their mother soothes him and tells him of course
not, that his sister was just making it up, she doesn't
really know everything. That was my first story.

Soon after that my mother, weary of my unruly frizz
and the tears at shampoo time, cut my hair close to my
head. If I tried letting it grow out my father would

mock me at dinner, telling me I looked like a sheep dog and to get it cut. I wore it short for many years, like my four brothers, like a fifth son.

In the stories I told in my head my hair was long and straight and glossy. In the sixties, when the fashion was for hair like Cher's used to be—a heavy curtain down to her knees—I spent hours of misery putting chemical straighteners on my hair, only to have it flame out around my head like the burning bush. Now that I'm post-menopausal, the traditional time when women become witches, my hair has lost its zip; it's thin and lanky and I would love to have my wild halo restored. I suppose that is the nature of the unsatisfied life, always to want what isn't possible.

Jewish friends of mine who grew up in larger communities tell of being taunted for having "mattress heads." The first time I heard this, I imagined heads covered in grey-and-white striped ticking; I didn't realize it was an insult, tossed at both Jews and Blacks, meaning our hair had the wiry quality of mattress stuffing. In my small town, no one called me that. My loathing was mostly internally induced, by parental strictures, and by isolation from the larger world; I came to adulthood feeling that a glass wall separated me from the universe of people who knew how to act, dress, feel pleasure. Even today, I often feel numb and bewildered. I try to believe it's the result of my isolated upbringing, but it's hard to believe that, deep down, I'm not a monster, a *lusus naturae*.

My parents, both desperately needy, unable to help each other, laid on me, their only daughter, the role of domestic support. My mother was bitter over opportunities lost or denied and took a savage delight in the failures of other women. Such failures proved to her that she had been defeated by the System, not by her own fears or withdrawals from life. Accepted into medical school in 1941, when that door was closed to many women, she chose not to take the bus from her home town to the University of Illinois on the day she needed to report to class. She could never explain why she did that, only giving a rambling tale of expecting more from the school than being consigned to a bus journey. If I brought home any achievement from school, she was almost savage in her bitterness. I quickly learned to keep success to myself.

Afraid of women and of female sexuality, my father, who thought it funny to wear a button demanding repeal of the 19th Amendment—which had granted US women suffrage in 1920—actually imputed minor witchlike powers to me. I could change traffic lights, for instance; my Gorgon stare could freeze men. I could do nothing to make myself an equal person.

Male writers such as Sartre and Bellow have recorded knowing early in life that their destiny lay in literature. Bellow knew he was "born to be a performing and interpretive creature," Sartre that he was born for words.

I call myself a writer, but I do so without great conviction. Where did they get this sense, I wonder? Like them, I wrote from an early age, but I knew that as in all fields literature belonged to men. The history and biography we studied in school told tales of the deeds of men. We learned to speak of the aspirations of mankind and of "man's inhumanity to man"—his inhumanity to woman not being worth recording.

The literature we studied was all written by men. If they were like me Bellow and Sartre may not even have known that women wrote in a serious way, that the first novelist to treat psychology as a significant force in human life was a woman. Sartre claims his boyhood was spent with Flaubert, Cornelius, Homer, Shakespeare; Bellow, that he turned to Anderson, Dreiser, Edgar Lee Masters, Vachel Lindsay (I do always wonder about such grandiose reports. Like politicians on the morning shows who say they had yogurt and granola for breakfast when they were really eating fried eggs and bacon, was Bellow in fact lost in the Tom Swift tales?)

The books Sartre's grandmother read were feminine, he says, and he was taught by his grandfather to deem them inferior. By an odd chance I learned the same lesson. We studied only one novel by a woman in my school—and her first name was George.

While Sartre's mother fueled his childish ambitions by binding his writings and forcing them on the neighbors ("*Regardez, how my Jean-Paul is a writer!*"), all my childhood dreams were directed to the present, specifically to escaping it, until I learned escape wasn't possible. My older brother and I would look at a picture of a ship at sea or a beautiful island, some strange wonderful place we wished to be. We would hold hands and run toward the picture and, by wishing hard enough, be transported into it. More often we climbed onto the two hitching posts in front of our house—remnants of the days when visitors had horses to tie up. After turning around three times we jumped, landing in a magic world where we fought dragons and elves came to our rescue.

The walls of my bedroom were papered with cabbage roses and behind the roses lay an imagined corridor, a long hall whose windows looked on perpetual sunlight. After going to bed I would escape into this corridor and live a life of total secrecy.

Little Women was the staple of my childhood, the book of girls, maternal love, women's friendship. I read *Little Women* for the first time when I was eight, and out of school for three weeks with measles. I wept copiously over Beth, I worried about Jo's temper, envied her for her attic room with its tin desk and pet rat, was put off by Amy and her stuck-up ways, and wished ardently, not just for a mother like Marmee, but for the rational calm of the March household.

I revisited *Little Women* dozens of times in the next ten years. The book drew me for many reasons. Despite their earnest efforts to follow the progress of Bunyan's pilgrim, the March sisters are no plaster saints. Each struggles with serious flaws—Jo's temper, Meg's vanity, Amy's greed, Beth's fear. They love and support each other, but also have the kinds of fights only siblings can produce. Indeed, their occasional fights make their intimacy more welcome. Their quarrels could assume alarming proportions, as when Amy burns Jo's only copy of her stories, the careful rewriting of many years' work. In retaliation, Jo lets Amy skate to her near-death in a spot on the river where Jo knows the ice is thin. I never thought Marmee made Amy express as much remorse as she should have—Jo had to assume an outsize mantle of contrition over her sister's accident—but Amy was alive. Jo's work was gone forever.

Looking back, I realize that among the things which drew me to the March sisters was just that: their sisterhood. Sisterhood allowed them to fight, make up, share each other's concerns. This was an intimacy missing from my own life. I have four brothers, but no sisters. (My mother also modeled herself, very consciously, not on Marmee, but on Don Marquis's Mehitabel; she would look at us and snarl, "What did I do to deserve all those damned kittens?")

As a child I missed having someone who shared my most personal interests, not to mention my fears. If I wanted to play with my brothers, I had to act out the Korean war, not play dress-up. While I loved baseball, I liked dolls, too. (My two-room country school fielded a team in our rural league; the high point of my childhood was getting picked to play third base, which I did with more zeal than skill—I think my lifetime batting average was .078.) If I had anxieties about school, love, or friendship, not to mention my temper, vanity, or the terrifying ballooning of my breasts when I turned thirteen, no one around me cared.

My parents lived five miles outside the town of Lawrence, Kansas, and the hours I didn't spend in school were at home, cleaning the house, doing dishes, acting as *de facto* nanny for my youngest brothers. Every Saturday, from the time I was seven until I left home, I did a baking for my father and brothers. My brothers were allowed to borrow the family car but I was a girl; I belonged at home. As a result, I grew up in an isolated world, one where I longed both for the intimacy of a lover, and the intimacy of a friend. The March sisters, with their Pickwick club, their nature walks, their attentive mother, had a life that I envied, and idealized.

Little Women also presented me with something less positive: a seduction into womanly self-denial. Among the novel's subtexts is the notion that women have, or ought to have, a self-sacrificing nature, that they should subdue their ambitions to domestic responsibilities. Beth is depicted as a household saint, the embodiment of this negative ideal; one might say that's what kills her.

Jo, who is a projection of Alcott herself and has the novel's leading voice, exemplifies that self-sacrifice in a more subtle fashion. Jo is a writer. At the end of Part II, she is married, with two sons, running a boarding school for boys in Aunt March's old mansion.

She and her sisters are discussing the dreams of being artists they had had in adolescence, and Jo says, "The life I wanted then seems selfish, lonely and cold to me now. I haven't given up the hope that I can write a good book yet, but I can wait . . . ." Amy, who paints and sculpts, responds that she still longs to create great original work, despite the importance of her domestic duties.

The conflict both sisters express was present in Alcott's life, in a deeper, more tormented form: her writing supported her family, including her father, who was aloof from such commonplace activities as making money. While in one sense Alcott fulfilled the artistic life Jo only aspired to, her artistry in a perverse way was a further enthrallment to domesticity. Her very words, that is, her inner-most self, were sacrificed to meet the needs of her family.

There's no evidence that Lizzie, the sister on whom Beth was modeled, was a domestic saint. Unlike the other three Alcott sisters, however, she did stay home, and she did die young, probably of anorexia exacerbated by an addiction to laudanum. (Anorexia was often praised by Victorian writers as the ultimate sign of a womanly self-denying nature.)

I was drawn in an uneasy way both to Jo, and to Beth. I've never met another lover of *Little Women* who admired Beth, but given the circumstances in which I lived, it was perhaps not surprising that I was attracted by an ideal of self-immolation. I was an angry, restless adolescent, wanting what I was told I couldn't have, but I also kept trying to lose my sense of self in high ideals of service.

The larger society in which I came of age didn't offer much in the way of a competing vision for girls. In Kansas during the fifties, in a society where everyone had a defined place, where everyone knew right from wrong, and what happened when you forgot, girls often saw limited horizons in their future.

I grew up in a world where white, Republican, Protestant male decision makers ("deciders," as we have recently learned to call them) were so much the norm that any questioning of this standard produced an aggressive reaction. Nowhere in the country, not even in Berkeley or Madison, was the reaction to the women's movement, the Civil Rights movement, or the anti-war movement as violent as it was in my home town.

For a fifteen-month span in 1970–71, there was a fire-bombing every day, often more than one. Student protestors set off some of these bombs; Minutemen and other right-wing groups carried out other attacks. The Minutemen were one of the earliest of the armed militias which are now widespread throughout America, particularly in rural states (Timothy McVeigh, who carried out the Oklahoma City bombing, had trained with a right-wing militia in rural Michigan). In 1970, the Minutemen tried to capitalize on student unrest in Lawrence by creating an atmosphere of fear great enough for the town to welcome an authoritarian government. To the town's credit, this did not happen, but the discovery that prominent local citizens were behind some of the attacks did cause the police to investigate rather charily.

I had left Lawrence for Chicago by then, so I don't know how widely or deeply the anti-war, pro Civil Rights movements altered institutions at the grass-roots level. When I was in school, we had mandatory daily Protestant prayers. Every Easter, the high school held a religious revival in the school auditorium; again, attendance was compulsory. In 1964, when a handful of brazen protestors (which included me, three Catholic girls, and one boy) claimed First Amendment protection against attendance, we were locked in a small room next to the principal's office during the revival service. What they would have done in event of a fire, I don't know—maybe rejoiced in the destruction of the heathen.

My school barred black students from college-track courses, while the town made sure they couldn't swim in the public pools. Realtors followed unwritten zoning proscriptions, consigning blacks and Jews to parts of town where houses often had dirt floors and no running water. My parents opted out of this world by buying an old farmhouse outside town, but they also became active campaigners for open housing.

The sexual politics of the fifties meant that abortion was a crime, and unmarried women had no access to contraception. Still, we were brought up to think that only bad girls had sex outside marriage—whereupon they reaped the inevitable punishment of pregnancy. Today, it is alarming to see that the triumphant religious right is proving very successful in returning us to that era.

My family was not unique in seeing my future as limited. What was unusual was the isolation and constraint in which I grew up. My parents were highly educated, and highly literate. Education and devotion to the written word were perhaps their highest values. My father, who was a research scientist, could read Greek, as well as German and Yiddish, and my mother was deeply and widely read in fiction and history.

But while they borrowed money to send my brothers to expensive schools far from home, they told me that if I wanted a college education, it would be at my own expense, and, further, that they would not permit me to leave Kansas. I was a National Merit scholar, but they had so inculcated in me my low self-valuation that I acquiesced in both strictures. When I finally started graduate work at the University of Chicago in 1968, my father told me not to be surprised if I failed, since it was a first-rate school and mine was a second-rate mind. There are still days when that criticism starts to sink me, and I lack the energy to rise above it.

My parents probably needed a kind of nurturing that

neither had received as children. My grandmothers were essentially orphans: my mother's mother died giving birth to her, my father's was sent to New York from eastern Europe after her own father was murdered in a pogrom when she was twelve. She became a mother at fifteen, and raised her children far from any support network—indeed, she never saw her own mother or most of her siblings again; they perished in the Holocaust.

These two women, my grandmothers, stumbled through maternity as best they could, but my parents went into family life without having much to give each other, let alone their five children. I've thought in my own later adulthood that my father and mother both wanted a mother so desperately that they tried to make me assume that role in their lives. When my mother used to visit me in Chicago, she would sit in the car, calling to me, "Pick me up, carry me inside; I'm just a helpless little girl."

In the larger world, they actively worked for social justice—my father brought Asian and African-American graduate students to his department at the University of Kansas in those segregated times; my mother supported the city's first African-American school teacher in his quest for decent housing.

Inside the home, my parents were insatiably needy, both too much to help each other. Their early years together were filled with witty conversation, dinners with interesting visitors from around the world. Later, sadly, drunkenness, blind rages, squalor, and worse horrors began to replace shared story telling, sports, jokes, and candle-lit dinners. Whatever the cause, it was a hard way for all of us to live.

Both my parents had stories to tell, their sides in an unending feud, one which grew more violent and more consuming as time passed, so that when my father was suffering from advanced dementia, my mother thought he was smirking at her, planning a new round of insults.

Despite these difficult years, and difficult lessons, my four brothers and I gained some good lessons, as well. My brothers and I all acquired a great love of books and language from them.

In addition, we learned about the importance of service for the public good. My father's parents met walking a picket line for the International Ladies Garment Workers Union. My grandfather was a cutter, my grandmother a finisher in a shirtwaist factory. Both hoped to improve the loathsome conditions in New York's sweatshops. One of my father's uncles was active enough in the Wobblies to be deported during the infamous Palmer raids of the 1920s.

My mother's father was the doctor in the small Illinois town where she grew up. He refused a job offer from the Mayo Clinic at the height of the Great Depression because he would not leave his community without medical care. He died at the age of fifty-one; he was recovering from surgery, but the old man who had trained him had fallen on the ice, and my grandfather went out into the snow to carry him to bed. My grandfather died shortly after that from the exertion this put on his heart, but seventy years later, people in his small community remember his service and his charity.

It was years before I learned a name for the domestic model in which I was reared, but in reading Virginia Woolf and Elizabeth Barrett Browning, I found I had grown up under the wings of the Angel in the House. This is the formal name for an unnatural vision of women described by Coventry Patmore in his 1854 eulogy to his wife's self-abnegating nature. Even without Patmore's name for her, this angel has blighted women's lives for a long time ("he for God only," Milton wrote of Adam and Eve, "she for God in him").

The struggle with the angel was a constant for nineteenth-century writers. Elizabeth Barrett Browning confronts her head-on in "Aurora Leigh," her epic about a woman who heroically finds her poetic voice. Barrett Browning, escaping her father's house for Italy with Robert, living there an extraordinary second life as the friend and chronicler of Italian revolutionaries, and as a vehement anti-slavery advocate, may have done better than most in ridding herself of this monstrous spirit.

On the other hand, I have an uneasy feeling that the angel helped kill that very gifted novelist, Elizabeth Gaskell. In addition to writing such important works as

Mary Barton and *North and South*, Gaskell was a devoted mother. She kept up a major correspondence with a wide circle of friends (including French and German scientists), ran social welfare programs in Manchester—and died of heart failure at fifty-five. That she wrote any fiction at all seems unbelievable; that she wrote four major novels—novels which deserve pride of place with *Bleak House* or *David Copperfield* for their powerful social commentary—is truly "a staggering work of heartbreaking genius."

In a world where women's roles were narrowly defined, Victorian writers sought ways either to retreat from these definitions, or to find other sources of nurture and recognition. Illness was one escape route: taking to bed seemed to be a useful strategy for Victorian artists trying to avoid a life of domestic slavery: Barrett Browning did it, and the great writer-explorer Isabella Bird was always so ill in her father's Edinburgh house that she couldn't get out of bed—until the day came to board a trans-Atlantic steamer once again. Bedridden, she died at home in 1904 at the age of seventy-three; if she'd headed to Antarctica, she might have lived another twenty years. Emily Dickinson avoided domestic responsibilities by hiding in cupboards. I've always admired the enterprise of these pioneering women.

In "Professions for Women," Woolf says the domestic angel also hovered between herself and her vocation as a writer. She describes the angel as "Intensely sympathetic. She was utterly unselfish. She sacrificed herself daily . . . she never had a mind or a wish of her own, but . . . sympathized always with the minds and wishes of others . . . ." The angel told Woolf:

> "Be tender, flatter, deceive, use all the arts and wiles of our sex. Never let anybody guess that you have a mind of your own. Above all, be pure." [Woolf says she] turned on the angel, caught her by the throat, and did my best to kill her . . . had I not killed her . . . she would have plucked the heart out of my writing.

Unfortunately, the wretched angel didn't die so easily, for Woolf, or the rest of us. She has very long wings which keep flapping over us. The contemporary rock/folk singer Jonatha Brooke even sings, "*I cannot kill the angel in the house.*"

Contemporary moral and political pundits proclaim that women's failure to meet the angel's high domestic standard has caused the fall of America. Former Republican Whip Tom DeLay blamed the shootings at Columbine High School on two things: teaching evolution in the schools, and women working outside the home. After the World Trade Center was attacked, religious figures on the Republican right announced that God was punishing America for, among other things, the women's liberation movement.

The angel kept me from a sense of a writer's vocation, or, indeed, any vocation when I was a child, and she still comes flying around my head, telling me not to be selfish, to give myself over to domestic or public duties first, that my writing, like Jo March's, can wait.

In the diaries of Midwestern farmwomen from the 1880s through the 1930s, their loneliness is a topic they revert to constantly: their loneliness, and the fact that their life on the farm was one of unremitting drudgery. With no one to talk to, no one to enter into their concerns or understand their needs, they often became psychotic. In fact, during that period, there was something of an epidemic of farmwomen burning down their own homes, often killing husbands, children and themselves in the process.

I wasn't so lonely that I had to burn down the farmhouse where I grew up, but I was lonely enough to turn to fiction for my friends. I had that imaginary inner life that I suppose helped me become a writer, but it wasn't a very comfortable place to live. I didn't have the kind of enterprise that sent Barrett Browning or Isabella Bird to their beds, but I did retreat into daydreams, a world of interior narrative: as I washed dishes, I was a Russian scientist pretending to be a dishwasher while hiding from the KGB, or I was the improbable beloved of an improbably urbane British nobleman—someone along the lines of Percy Blakeney. Sometimes my dreams seemed so real that I could spend a whole day inside them, not noticing where I was or what I was doing.

When I was a teenager, both parents wanted to use my words to make their points—my mother demanding poems describing her entrapment, my father stories proclaiming his unlauded glories. I dutifully created both. But beyond that my writing roused so little interest that my mother told me my father burned all my childhood papers in some housekeeping frenzy or other. I kept hoping she got it wrong. Before they died, I spent hours hunting through their attic for some story, some diary, a remnant to connect me with my past, something that might tell me what dreams I used to have. Nothing comes to light.

How did I survive this upbringing? How did I become a writer?

These were questions that I tried to answer for an essay in a collection called *Family Portraits*, published by Doubleday in 1985. In company with writers far more distinguished—I. B. Singer, for one—I was asked to write about the family member who most influenced and supported my writing voice. I thought of my mother, who was a great reader and story teller, I thought of my older brother, who taught me to read and write, but I could think of no family member who cared that I wrote. Instead, my fantasy of writing had been a daydream so private I never shared it with anyone. So I wrote an essay about my Golden Retriever Capo, who stayed with me day and night while I labored on my first novel. Doubleday didn't want an essay about a dog.

I thought again, and wrote about my mother's cousin Agnes. Doubleday liked Agnes, and included her in the collection.

Among other things, I wrote:

The summer I turned ten, on one of her abrupt visits, Agnes learned I was writing a story. She asked me to read it to her. She sat in the living room and listened with total attention. It still seems unbelievable to me that a grown woman could really *want* to spend an hour hearing a young girl read a story. She didn't offer any literary criticism. I don't even remember her saying anything. Just that she sat and listened . . .

Agnes's listening to one story was not enough to give me a sense that my future lay in words. It was enough, though, to keep me writing. After Agnes listened to my story I would lie in bed imagining my parents dead and me adopted by her, taken into her school where there were only girls.

The dream took on new dimensions in 1958, when we moved to our house in the country. At first I loved it: I finally had my own room and we went to a two-room country school—just like in *Understood Betsy* or *On the Banks of Plum Creek*. Later I came to hate it. My parents' fights intensified and the isolation of the country made it easy to seal me off completely from friends my own age, from any activities but school and housework.

The main line of the Santa Fe crossed the road at the bottom of the hill on the outskirts of Lawrence. There wasn't any crossing gate or bell and every now and then the Kansas City Chief, roaring around a blind curve toward San Francisco, would annihilate a family.

Mary and Dave would be fighting, not paying attention to the road or to the tracks. The crash would be appalling. We'd be at the house, of course, my four brothers and I, lounging around reading or maybe playing softball. We should have been doing a dozen chores—mowing the lawn (my older brother's job), vacuuming (mine), changing the baby's diapers (mine again) or sorting the bottles in the trash to take to the dump (my brother). I don't need a dishwasher, Mary used to tell visitors—I have two right here. And she would point at my older brother and me.

When we heard the car in the drive we leaped into action, attacking our chores—there was hell to pay if we were found loafing in bourgeois self-indulgence. And then we saw it was the sheriff's car, the red light flashing. We raced over to see what he wanted, me grabbing the baby and carrying him along on my hip.

The sheriff looked at us very kindly. He said maybe we should go sit down: he had something very serious to tell us. There'd been an accident and we were orphans now. Was there someone we could call to look after us? Of course not, we already did any looking after there was to do, but we couldn't tell him that, and anyway, we were underage, we needed guardians.

I would go to Agnes, to the school for irremediable girls. Even though she only took girls I would have to bring the two little boys with me, they were mine to look after (they thought I was their mother. When they started kindergarten they didn't know what the word "sister" meant—they didn't know that was me: they thought they had two mothers.).

We looked solemnly at the sheriff, conjuring up tears out of shock, but we couldn't believe it had really happened: we were really orphans. Just like *Anne of Green Gables* or *English Orphans*. Our future changed miraculously.

And then Mary and Dave would come up the drive, still arguing, not dead at all, and we would leap into activity that was never quite frenzied enough. My older brother could never get tasks quite right, or the tasks set for him would change between when they were assigned and when he did them, and most of the yelling went his way. The rest of us slid upstairs.

I want to say here what I couldn't say in 1985: there was no cousin Agnes. The behaviors, and support, I ascribed to Agnes were an amalgam of my teachers and friends, as well as some adult women whom I saw interact with my parents. However, Agnes did have a very particular existence: she was my imaginary mentor.

She came to me in the winter of 1969, during my first year of graduate school at the University of Chicago, when I shared a slum with three other students. I was twenty-one then, fat, ungainly, painfully lonely, so fearful of criticism that I seldom spoke in my classes. I'd never had a boyfriend and aside from my three room-mates I didn't have women friends in Chicago, either. My room-mates and I shared a dismal apartment on the south side—six rooms for a hundred-sixty-five dollars a month and all the cockroaches we could eat. We killed two hundred and fifty of them one night, spraying the oven where they nested and stomping on them when they scampered out. (You'd have to be twenty-one to want to count the bodies.)

It was never warmer than fifty-five in the building and that was a most bitter winter. The city code says it has to be at least sixty-two during the day. We'd get building inspectors out who would solemnly measure the air. Then they'd learn the landlady worked as a precinct captain for the Daley machine and their thermometer miraculously would register fifteen degrees higher than ours.

I had gone to Kansas for the winter holiday. As usual on my visits, my mother became drunk and angry, and my father retreated into a menacing silence—he sometimes went as much as three days without speaking, but his silent presence was filled with a ferocious anger that dominated the house around him.

I fled back to Chicago several days before the end of the winter holiday, while my room-mates were still out of town. Carrying my heavy suitcase up the stairs to the apartment entrance I blundered into the doorjamb,

knocking the wind out of myself. I dumped my suitcase
down and sat on it, not even going inside, so miserable
with my fat, my clumsiness, my loneliness that I hoped
I might just die right there.

My two youngest brothers would care, of course, as
would my friend Kathleen, but my parents wouldn't
even come to the funeral. I'd been active in social
justice work both in Chicago and Lawrence; admiring
community leaders came to the service to pay me
homage. In my coffin I looked like a Botticelli angel,
miraculously slender with long soft golden curls. The
picture brought a lump to my throat.

At that moment, Agnes came to me. Her name was
Agnes Bletch; she ran a finishing school for irremediable girls, girls like me, who always spilled food on
themselves while eating, and ran into doorjambs more
often than they walked through doorways.

Agnes's school didn't do the impossible. She didn't
train girls to eat tidily, or walk like Audrey Hepburn.
Instead, she taught her students to spill food on
themselves with so much *élan* that every other woman
in the room poured soup down her dress, hoping to look
half as good as the Bletchites.

It was a long slow journey I started that January
afternoon, a journey to my voice. It took another decade
of writing privately, not showing my work to anyone,
before I began to try to write for publication. Without
the women's movement, without my mentor and friend
Isabel Thompson, who took me under her wing the

following fall, and without the support of Courtenay Wright, whom I later married, I might never have had the courage to write publicly.

The people who made up my cousin Agnes included my fourth-grade teacher, Patti Shepherd. She did, indeed, urge me to read my stories to her during the summer of 1957. She made me feel my stories meant something. My high school teachers Jayanne Angell and Bill Mullins both told me I had a gift with language; they gave me a spark of confidence in my writing, one that sent me to New York the summer of 1970, when I was twenty-three, to try to get a job in the magazine world. I failed dismally at that and returned to Chicago, but their encouragement did keep me writing—stories, poetry—all very privately for myself until I was in my early thirties and finally had the confidence to try to write my first novel.

The adult women I watched as a child included my Aunt Mary Clare, whom my father both flirted with and was afraid of. She was a general's daughter, and ruled her household with a feminine but firm discipline. When my uncle was stationed at Ft. Leavenworth, forty-five miles from us, they visited often. As a child, I saw how Mary Clare could charm—and intimidate— my terrifying father into behaving like a civilized person with his family.

Finally, Emily Taylor, the dean of women at the University of Kansas, where I was an undergraduate, played a strong role in starting me on the road to rethinking where I belonged on the planet. I attended the university partly with money I had started earning at age thirteen, when I took a job as a dishwasher in a science lab, and partly with scholarships I was awarded. The most important of these scholarships was named for Elizabeth Watkins, who had to quit school at thirteen to look after her siblings and her father, and who left the fortune she later acquired to support women students.

One fall night in 1964, when Dr. Taylor hosted a dinner for the Watkins scholars, she asked us what we planned to do with our educations. During my whole life, no adult had ever asked me what I wanted to be when I grew up. I knew that I was destined for marriage and motherhood. Indeed, my parents' goals for me were so limiting that they sent me through secretarial training so that I could find a job if I didn't marry right away. So when this formidable woman asked us what we wanted to do with our lives, I went numb: I didn't have an answer. Many of the scholars in the room were in the same boat; we all stammered about wanting to be better wives and mothers.

There's an early episode in *Doonesbury* when Joanie Caucus has run away from her husband and ends up at Walden. This goes back to the seventies, to women's first tentative steps in looking for jobs, equity and self-esteem, and Joanie—these days a successful lawyer—had never worked outside the home. She gets a job in a daycare center.

One day she asks the kids what they want to be when they grow up. The boys choose astronauts, cowboys, firemen. The girls raise their arms and cry with one voice, "We want to be mommies." Joanie looks at the class and says, "Boys, leave us. The girls and I are going to have a talk."

Like Joanie Caucus, Emily Taylor said, "Girls, we're going to have a talk." She said, "The University is not investing resources in your education so you can stay home; we expect you to make a contribution to society. Your education matters for what you do with it, and what it does for you, not for some man and his unborn children." That was an exhilarating and frightening night for me, that first night an important adult expected me to do something serious with my life.

That night in 1964, the Civil Rights Act, with its empowering Title VII legislation, was barely two months old. We were all taking baby steps toward the future that fall. Billie Jean King, *Roe. v Wade*, Justices Thurgood Marshall and Sandra Day O'Connor, even V I Warshawski, were a long way off. It was my great good fortune to come of age just when America became a land of great possibility and opportunity. For the next decade, I rode on the waves of that wonderful revolution.

2

The King and I

On Saturday, August 6, 1966, Chicago's near west side was as quiet as the small Kansas town where I grew up. Quieter, in fact: George, Barbara, and I, roaming the neighborhood, were the only people on the streets. The five-room bungalows, the south side's signature residence, were empty behind their lacy curtains. Even the children, who usually swarmed the streets and play lots, had disappeared.

We three were nineteen, college volunteers in a summer program run by the Presbyterian church of Chicago. We'd been assigned to manage a summer day camp for kids seven to eleven years old in a mostly Catholic, Polish-Lithuanian part of the city. The neighborhood, called Gage Park, lay south of "Back of the Yards," home to the stockyards made famous in Upton Sinclair's *The Jungle*. Gage Park's streets were lined with brick bungalows; many of our families had moved to them as a first step up the housing ladder from the uninsulated clapboard apartments in Back of the Yards.

Like me, George and Barbara had come to Chicago from agricultural states. Despite any reading we might have done—and the city's Democratic machine had

been a textbook study of corrupt government in my
high school—we were profoundly ignorant about the
city we would encounter that summer. Nothing we read
in a civics textbook could have prepared us for understanding the complicated passions and needs in the
community we served. What we brought to Chicago,
besides our ignorance, was a passion for service and
social justice, and the boundless energy and optimism
of our generation.

The whole country was in turmoil that summer. The
decade of Civil Rights activism sparked by the Mont-
gomery bus boycott had led to major legal and legis-
lative victories, but hadn't changed a lot of reality on
the ground. Segregation, as well as economic and
education discrimination, were facts of life from Boston
to Birmingham. Race riots, student protests, Civil
Rights marches, anti-war protests, and the incipient
women's movement kept cities and universities in a
state of constant upheaval.

Racists and segregationists kept telling us that "you
can't legislate morality," meaning we should wait another few centuries for racism to work its way out of the
American psyche, instead of trying to correct four
centuries of damage in the present.[1]

Chicago, with its large African-American population,
had been dubbed the most segregated city in America.
Until passage of the 1964 Civil Rights act, African-
Americans couldn't shop in many downtown stores.
Students in Chicago's black communities were sent to

school in trailers because the city wouldn't put up new schools or fix up old ones in those neighborhoods. In Chicago, as in my home town, black students were often barred from college preparatory courses. A Chicago friend of mine who dreamed of medical school was told by her high school she could have a future as a radiology technician and not to try to get into science classes. Still denied access to most Lake Michigan beaches, black children also didn't have swimming pools in their badly-kept neighborhood parks.

Blacks weren't allowed to drive buses or elevated trains, or even garbage trucks. At City Hall, they could work only as janitors, and even then, for a fraction of what white workers earned. Trade unions were segregated, with black workers confined to the most difficult jobs, and allotted a lower pay scale than whites.

George, Barbara, and I were eager to right all these wrongs. When we arrived in the city in June, we were miffed that we'd been sent to what looked to us like a backwater of the Civil Rights struggle. We wanted to be on the black south side, where a charismatic white Presbyterian minister named John Fry was politicizing the street gangs. Over time, he helped turn the Blackstone Rangers, a street-gang that specialized in extortion and fighting, into the Black P Stone Nation. Ten years later, the gang morphed into the El Rukns, a Mafia-style organization that controlled gambling, prostitution and drug sales in a big chunk of the city. In the seventies and eighties, when most of the top El Rukns were behind bars, they intimidated and bribed sheriff's deputies and ended up essentially controlling the prisons where they were incarcerated (the El Rukns controlled narcotic traffic within the prisons themselves, and often used drugs as bribes with prison personnel).

However, in 1966 it seemed daring and glamorous for Mr. Fry to give them meeting space in the church, and to let them store their weapons in its auditorium. His church was part of the Black Power movement, and we wanted to be part of it, too.

When we arrived in the city, we didn't know our assignment would put us at the center of a less glamorous, but more important part of the Civil Rights movement: Martin Luther King had arrived in Chicago in January, moving into a tenement building in the black neighborhood adjacent to Gage Park, divided from us by Ashland Avenue. In the rigid segregation of those days, all housing on the west side of Ashland and beyond was white; all housing on the east side and beyond was black.

King was spending a summer trying to help Chicago's black community figure out a way to tackle Chicago's terrible history of housing, education, and pay inequities. And on August 6, he and other Civil Rights leaders were leading a protest march in nearby Marquette Park, a park which refused to let black children swim in the south side's only good pool, or play on its beautifully maintained golf course and baseball fields.

Everyone in the city knew that King's march would lead to violence in Marquette Park. I don't think anyone knew how ugly it would be: white mobs torching cars, throwing rocks and Molotov cocktails, hitting out with motorcycle chains, while the police and fire departments, all-white forces who had grown up on the south side—and who knew many of the mob members by name—would absorb physical and verbal abuse for protecting Dr. King.

Tom Phillips, pastor at the church where we were working, had ordered us university volunteers to stay away from Marquette Park. One July afternoon, after our workday ended, we had gone to Soldier Field to hear Dr. King, and then had marched behind him to City Hall, where, evoking his namesake, he taped a list of demands to Mayor Daley's door.

In our own neighborhood, we had spent June and July immersing ourselves in Gage Park life: we attended youth meetings at St. Justin Martyr, the local Catholic church, where we were startled to find college students who were violently racist, speaking in the crudest language about Dr. King: we had naively assumed every person in our generation was as fired up as we were by the need for change. We had gone to meetings of Gage Park's White Citizens Council and read the hate literature they were handing out.

We had tried to counter the messages our children were receiving at home with study programs on living together in harmony, with songs about "Black and white and yellow and brown/Altogether built this town," and "This land is your land, this land is my land." We thought we had earned the right to take part in the August 6 march.

Tom Phillips knew that we were eager for martyrdom, eager to show our real commitment to civil rights by getting arrested, since that was the sign that you were truly part of the movement. In retrospect, I think, too, that Tom worried about our safety: the march was the culmination of a month of horrible violence on the south side, where white mobs yelling such slogans as "Burn them like the Jews" and "The only way to end n—s^2 is to exterminate them," fired rockets and threw bricks at blacks attempting to march on realtors who wouldn't show houses to black or mixed-race couples. At any rate, we loved and respected Tom, and reluctantly followed his edict.

As the violent day unfolded, Barbara, George, and I did play one small role in curtailing the mayhem. In our mostly Catholic neighborhood, two thousand people attended mass every Sunday at St. Justin Martyr. The week before the march, the pastors had preached that open housing and racial tolerance were part of Christ's commandment to love one another—a sermon which caused attendance to drop to 200 for the rest of the summer.

As my co-workers and I paced the streets, we came on a fire at St. Justin's. Angry parishioners had banked carpets around the foundation of the rectory, and set fire to them. We grabbed the carpets in our bare hands, oblivious of the fire, of our own bare legs and sandal-shod feet, and carried them to the asphalt of the playground where we beat out the flames.

This was a small action indeed on a day where a mob of 2500 surrounded police cars and upended them, beat up cops and nuns alike for protecting or standing with the demonstrators, burnt cars, and even hurled insults at the Catholic archbishop of Chicago, who had the guts and grace to stand with Dr. King. At the end of the day, Dr. King said, "I have never in my life seen such hate, not in Mississippi, or Alabama. This is a terrible thing."[3]

The roots of racial animosity on the South Side went back to the end of the nineteenth century. During the waves of black migration from the South in the two decades before World War I, white realtors and citizens worked together to restrict black housing to a narrow corridor about a mile west of Lake Michigan. Realtors had a written policy of subdividing existing homes into as many rooms as possible, to pack six or even ten people to a room, before they would allow blacks to move into an adjacent block. Blacks who bought or rented homes outside that strip were met with fires, bombs, and, in the race riots of 1919, roving white mobs who shot and lynched them.

The policy of redlining—outlining areas on maps in red where banks, realtors, and insurance companies would refuse to deal with black customers—was actually begun by the federal government in 1933. While the North looked contemptuously at the South's *de jure* segregation, northern cities embraced redlining with great eagerness.

George, Barbara, and I lived with white families in their small bungalows, bunking in attics turned into makeshift, immaculate spare bedrooms. George lived with a precinct captain who drove a garbage truck. Barbara and I shared an attic with the elder daughter of a family whose father drove a city bus; her mother baked cakes for a local supermarket chain. The younger child, who was severely retarded, slept in the dining room downstairs. The parents cared for her at home, without complaint or question, without any outside assistance. The racial strife of the summer affected them mostly as a worry: would they have to move, could they afford to move; if they stayed and the neighborhood became violent, how would they protect their feeble child?

The children in our day camp were often anxious: outings to the beach started with black children throwing stones as we waited at Ashland Avenue for the bus, and often ended with an emergency dash home before the next round of riots began. The first time we took the children to Wrigley Field to see a baseball game, they wouldn't sit next to a black person on the train, standing for the hour-long ride while half the seats in the car were empty. We told the kids they would forfeit the right to go on outings if they did it again, and, eyes wide with fear, they would perch on the edge of a seat, terrified of being assaulted by the tired middle-aged women next to them.

We counselors tried to soothe, we tried to teach, but probably too often we only preached. And, after all, we didn't have to stay on the south side when the summer ended; we were returning to school. In September, I myself went back to Kansas to finish my undergraduate degree.

That summer changed my life forever. I had gone to Chicago out of restlessness: big events were happening on the world stage and I wanted to be part of them. The riots, the marches that threatened Mayor Daley's legendary control over his city, that led to massive white flight to the suburbs, that exhausted Martin Luther King, that elevated the power of the black street gangs (they provided protection for Dr. King and his associates), that frayed the police to the breaking point—so that two years later they took out their frustrations on the anti-war protestors in front of the Democratic National Convention—seemed to me to be signs of change, even of hope.

Looking back on that time now, I think you had to be young to survive that era with hope. The Vietnam War was heating up, taking Lyndon Johnson's attention from civil rights to the war and the anti-war movement. The levels of hate and violence in the white communities of Chicago were echoed across the country in subsequent years. The Civil Rights movement itself was fragmenting among conflicting philosophies of non-violence, armed struggle, separatism, and many other factions. Already worn out by the demands on him, by the factionalization of the Civil Rights movement, as well as the relentless harassment of the FBI and racist groups, Dr. King was exhausted almost beyond bearing by the violence in Chicago.

Even so, I came away from my summer filled with the sense that change for good was possible, that if I and my peers put enough energy and good will into the struggle, we could transform America. And I felt that my destiny lay in Chicago.

When I finished my undergraduate degree and was at loose ends, not knowing what to do next, Tom Phillips and his wife invited me to stay with them while I found a paying job in the city. Later, I did a PhD in US history, trying to understand and come to terms with the roots of the misery playing out on the city's streets. (Although my dissertation, *The Breakdown of Moral Philosophy in New England before the Civil War* seems pretty far removed from Martin Luther King and Marquette Park, I wrote my master's thesis on the abolitionists and their connection to the religious movements of the 1840s.)

Later still, I created my Chicago investigator, V I Warshawski, who grew up in one of those five-room bungalows on the city's south side. Much of what shaped V I's history came out of the summer, including my trying to understand not just the city's racial divisions, but its ethnic and religious ones.

Chicagoans define themselves by the Catholic parish they grew up in, by the little square foot of Europe they came from. To this day, when I meet a native for the first time and they ask where I'm from, if I say "Kansas, but Chicago's been my home for forty years" they'll say impatiently, "no, where are you *from!*" meaning, what poverty-stricken corner of Europe did my ancestors flee—and don't I still feel a strong emotional bond to the lands of my grandparents' birth?

I gave V I a Polish surname, because one of my four grandparents did come from Poland, and I knew I couldn't write convincingly about black or Latina experience. But I'm not a native, and my work betrays that: after making V I's paternal grandfather a Polish immigrant, I never have her doing the stuff that locals do, going to Polish picnics, Krakow dance festivals, or the Pulaski Day parade.

I should have known I was doomed to ethnic ignorance from my first job: I was a secretary in the political science department at the University of Chicago. This is where I had my introduction to hyphenated Americans. Polish-American students expected me to waive fines for them, or get them into over-subscribed courses. When I wouldn't, they told me I was a traitor to the Polish nation. Adults, even those who've migrated to the suburbs, identify themselves with the neighborhoods of their childhood. When I worked as a marketing manager in the eighties, our group secretary, who came from the Irish south side, used to spit when she

talked about Irish staff from west side communities—
Black Irish she called them. She wouldn't even pass
along phone messages from them ("That Sandy Re-
illy," she'd snort, "he tried to interrupt you, but I made
sure he knew his place.")

Most of all, though, the summer of 1966 made me
aware of the issues of voice and voicelessness that
dominate my writing, because they dominate my emotional life.

Forty years ago, I felt, rather than understood, the
helplessness of the people I was living with. I didn't
then and don't now hold any brief for the fears that
turned into bottle-throwing, car-burning hate in Marquette Park that August day, or led whites to sell their
small homes at a loss and flee in terror for the western
suburbs. But in my youth and ignorance and arrogance,
I didn't understand that those five-room homes were
the only thing my host family and their neighbors
owned. I didn't understand the way the banks and
realtors, and the lending policies of the federal government, fanned the fires of fear to induce whites into
panic-selling at a loss, so that large institutions could
make a fortune on the turnaround in selling their
houses to a black family at an inflated price.

These days, when western newspapers express scorn
and pity toward Muslims induced to riot over Danish
cartoons by cynical mullahs or governments, I think of
the ease with which Chicago's hatemongers fanned the
flames on the Christian south side in the 1960s. (I even

think of the ease with which jingoist politicians and broadcasters roused some Americans to torch businesses with French names in the run-up to the invasion of Iraq.) None of us is immune to feeling helpless, impotent, and furious.

I'm not very interested in the needs or motivations of the meta-powerful, the Cheneys, the Halliburtons, the Enrons; it's a weakness in my books that I don't explore the characters of the wicked very well. I've always sided with the underdog, and my Chicago summer made the raw neediness of underdogs palpable to me.

In *Uncle Tom's Cabin*, the saintly little Eva St. Clair dies under the weight of the cruelty around her. When Eva hears a tale of terrible atrocities committed against a slave woman named Prue, "Her cheeks grew pale, and a deep, earnest shadow passed over her eyes." Later she tells her father, "These things sink into my heart."

When I was trying to think about how to discuss my novels and questions of social justice, I imagined myself with my hands pressed to my bosom, saying with a throbbing intensity, "These things sink into my heart." But I don't side with the underdog because I'm saintly like little Eva. I do so because I'm as needy as the most helpless.

I grew up in a tangled nest of outsideness. As the only girl in my family, I was constrained from the age of nine to give up my own childhood in becoming the caretaker of my young brothers. My family was one of the few Jewish families in the town of Lawrence—our arrival brought the number of Jewish men to ten so that the community could start holding services. We were like giraffes, an oddity that invited staring. I knew that if I revealed any of the ugliness of our home life to the larger world, and it was ugly in ways that are still hard for me to think about, I would be bringing shame to the Jews, who were beleaguered enough without my adding to their woes. The shadow of the Holocaust, in which my European family was obliterated down to the last infant cousin, lay heavy over my childhood: one did not make one's private woes a mocking point for gleeful Gentiles.

When my father gave my dolls and stuffed animals to my young brother, telling me that at nine I was too old for toys, my mother told me not to cry, because there were children in Harlem and Johannesburg, or dead children in the Vilna ghetto, who'd never even had toys.

My needs and desires were insignificant in the grand scheme of neediness—it was my job to serve, to help undo bonds of wickedness, share my bread with the hungry, and in general, let the oppressed go free. My life wasn't supposed to hold pleasure: my parents forbade art or music classes, any after-school groups, or outings with friends. Once, when I took part in a school play, my parents condemned my selfishness in language so scalding that they effectively kept me from any other leisure activities. Even today, if I sit in my attic writing on my novels, I feel guilty for not being out on the streets, immolating myself on the altar of social neediness. I should be tutoring, working for abortion rights, saving Darfur, undoing the Patriot Act—in short, saying yes to every appeal that crosses my desk. Only a selfish person would stay in her attic spinning stories.

I was a person raised to serve, who came of age in a time of passion for justice. My character dovetailed neatly with the times. My own sense of voicelessness also led me to see and feel the anguish of the powerless.

I had been writing since I was old enough to read, short stories that were, or at least tried to be, funny takes on the world around me, occasional mysteries, lots of fantasy. After my summer in Chicago, I started trying to write more naturalistic stories.

As a child, the worst thing about the Holocaust to me had been the thought of so many people dying nameless, without anyone remembering them. As a young adult, I had the same fear about the people I'd been working with. No one would remember their stories. It became my mission to do that.

Over the next decade, I kept trying to write little stories about the people, or the neighborhood, or the fears or the hatreds . . . A policeman on the L—Chicago's name for our rapid transit trains—who'd been on twenty-four-hour shifts for three days during one round of riots; he was nursing a single pink rosebud that he was taking home to his wife. His face was covered in dirt and stubble and cracking with fatigue, but his hands were gentle around the flower . . . A woman, mother of a co-worker, who had an order of protection against her

husband, and called us as well as the cops the afternoon
her husband showed up, trying to break in. The man had
gone without lunch for ten years to buy a Cadillac, which
he cherished above all else in his life; he was begging his
wife, through the window of their basement apartment,
to let him back inside. "I'll even let you drive my car,
honey," he offered. Those and hundreds more stories
like them, hard lives with heartbreaking moments—
these things sink into my heart.

Early on in my life in Chicago, I felt a special
fascination for the city's southeast side. South Chicago,
Pullman, the East Side are the main neighborhoods of
what used to be the heart of Chicago's industrial might;
it's there that V I Warshawski grew up, and there that
some of her most harrowing adventures occur.

When I first arrived in the city in 1966, we drove in
late at night through the steel mills. Methane flares,
street lights, factory lights, and over it all, the white-
orange fire of pouring steel, covered the landscape,
until the lights abruptly stopped at the inky vastness of
Lake Michigan at night. It looked like a prelude for the
entry into hell.

High wages in steel and allied industries brought
successive waves of immigrants to the mills in South
Chicago. They also brought successive waves of combat
to the area's streets: as Swedes gave way to Germans
and then to Poles, Serbs, and finally, Hispanics and
African-Americans, each racial/ethnic group fought the
newcomers, trying to protect their jobs.

Through my stepsons,[4] whose friendships spanned the south side, I got to know some of the teens from South Chicago. One of them was a small young woman, around eighteen, with red hair which she wore down to her knees. She liked to go into bars, get guys to buy her drinks, and then beat them up if they asked for sexual favors in return. She had learned fighting in the toughest streets in the city. When I created my detective in 1982, I wanted her to be a street-fighter, not an expert in some subtle martial art, so it was natural to turn to South Chicago for her roots.

The neighborhood has many other qualities that make it endlessly interesting. People and institutions there feel cut off from the city, and they tend to be loyal to one another and to the neighborhood (at least within their own ethnic enclaves). As the steel industry collapsed in the eighties, South Chicago and the surrounding areas lost almost 200,000 jobs, but the local banks tried for over a decade to carry customers struggling to make mortgage payments on their immaculate bungalows. However, by 1985, banks were discouraging prospective buyers from investing in the neighborhood.

Chicago is built on swamps; South Chicago holds the sole remains of the wetlands which used to stretch from Gary, Indiana twenty-five miles north to Chicago's Loop.[5] Sixty-five years ago much of this area, including the eight-lane highway that connects the south side with the Loop, was still under water. The marsh has long since been filled with everything from cyanide to slag, with a hundred million tons of garbage added to give it body.

The locals call the remaining bit of swamp Dead Stick Pond, from the eponymous rotting wood which dots it. It appears on no city maps. It is so obscure that Chicago police officers stationed ten blocks away at the Port of Chicago haven't heard of it. Nor have officials at the local Chicago Park District office.

Under skies purple-pink with smog, marsh grasses and cattails still tower above cars on the gravel roads that crisscross the swamp. Despite a century of dumping that has filled the ground water with more carcinogens than the EPA can classify, the grasses flourish. Purple-necked ducks continue to nibble at delicacies in the fetid water. Their families have come here for millennia, breaking the journey from Canada to the Amazon. It's a birdwatchers haven, but also a prime location for poachers trying to bag endangered birds—on a busy fall Saturday, you can find birdwatchers and fishers, perhaps also watch the badly over-stretched environmental police trying to catch poachers.

Conflicting signs tacked to the trees both proclaim the area a clean-water project and warn trespassers of hazardous wastes. Despite warning signs, on a good day you can find anything from a pair of boots to a bedstead dumped in Dead Stick Pond.

Fish have been returning to the Calumet River and its tributaries since passage of the Clean Water Act in the seventies, but the ones that make their way into the pond show up with massive tumors and rotted fins. The phosphates in the water further cut the amount of oxygen that can penetrate the surface. Even so, wild birds continue to land here on their migratory routes.

Chicagoans so poor they live in shanties without running water catch their dinners in the marsh. Their shacks dot unmarked trails in the swamps. The inhabitants have a high mortality rate from esophageal and stomach cancers because of the pollutants in their well water. The half-feral dogs around their homes make it hard for any social welfare agent to get a clear idea of their living situation.

I discovered Dead Stick Pond through two dedicated environmental activists who were trying to bring green jobs to the south side. When they reported that a mob-connected waste hauler was illegally dumping garbage into Dead Stick Pond, their lives were threatened. The Chicago state's attorney told them the city could only investigate if they were actually murdered, so the two women were forced to give up their jobs and move north—another story for V I to tackle some day.

V I has twice been left for dead in her old neighborhood, once in Dead Stick Pond itself (*Blood Shot*, 1988) and again in the landfill where the city dumps its ten thousand daily tons of garbage (*Fire Sale*, 2005).

Another oddity of the southeast side is the visibility of the city's archeological layers. Streets and sidewalks in this poverty-stricken area have collapsed in many places and the city takes a long time to make repairs here. If you look into the holes you'll see cobblestones five feet down. Because the landfill a century ago didn't hold back the underlying marshes the city jacked itself up and built another layer over the top. South Chicago is one of the few places where the original substratum shows through.

I used to take visiting journalists to the south side, to show them Dead Stick Pond and V I's childhood home, but lately, South Chicago has become home to the city's most violent murders. As the public housing projects near the city center have been torn down to make way for gentrification, their residents have been shipped out of sight to the city's southeast edge. The arrival of new street gangs has destabilized the neighborhood. The last time I drove down there, in 2004, our car was surrounded by an ugly group of gangbangers. We were saved by the presence of a friend, who knew the brother of one of the men and persuaded them to leave us alone.

My friend Dave, who saved me that day, is in a way a constant reproach to me. In the language of the streets, you can't talk the talk unless you walk the walk, and Dave definitely walks the walk. He worked for a decade in the mills, trying to organize clean union elections, was beaten within an inch of his life, stalked by the FBI, and then had his cervical vertebrae crushed in a rail mill accident. When US Steel closed down, Dave and a friend stayed on in South Chicago. They started a general contracting business and build homes and offices, with a specialty in ornamental ironwork. On the side, they run a jobs training program for youths in South Chicago who are now the third generation in their families unable to find work. Whenever I see Dave, I realize I need to be out on the street, doing something, instead of staying home, writing fiction. Failing that, I tell myself that my fiction mustn't stray too far from the issues of voice, power, and the lives of people who lack both.

I feel a fierce nostalgia for the sixties, a nostalgia like an insatiable hunger. Out on the streets, these were some of the ugliest times in American history, racism made naked for the whole country, indeed the whole world, to see. In the courts and in the White House, these were some of the noblest moments.

The President of the United States, speaking to the nation, talked about the centuries of harm white Americans had committed against black Americans. "Long years of degradation have broken apart Negro families on a massive scale." LBJ demanded support for affirmative action, saying that "You do not take a person who, for years, has been hobbled by chains, and . . . bring him up to the starting line of a race and then say 'you are free to compete' and still justly believe that you have been completely fair."

The President then challenged corporate leaders to create jobs for chronically unemployed teenagers. Johnson told them that St. Peter soon would ask "what you did with your affluence and what you did as a beneficiary of this great system of government."[6]

Living as I do now under a government that has
abrogated all responsibility for the needy of all ages and
races—for instance, cutting federal health insurance
benefits for young children and for veterans, refusing to
discuss an increase in the minimum wage[7]—while it has
operated brazenly and openly only for the benefit of its
corporate sponsors, it is hard not to feel despair.

The Attorneys-General of the Sixties, Robert Ken-
nedy and Nicholas Katzenbach, threw the weight of the
Department of Justice behind enforcement of the
Voting Rights Act and the Civil Rights Act of 1964.
The Attorneys-General of the new millennium, John
Ashcroft and Alberto Gonzalez, have crafted and en-
forced legislation that undoes the Bill of Rights and
removes the right of *habeas corpus*. Mr. Gonzalez has
written the legal opinions that support torture as an
instrument of my government's policy.

In Chicago, the angry white residents who rioted on
the south side in 1966 fled en masse to the western
suburbs, where they established a Republican organization every bit as powerful and ruthless as the old Daley
machine. Today they elect some of the most reactionary
Republicans in Congress.

The present government has gutted the Equal Em-
ployment Opportunity Commission, which was created
by President Johnson to handle questions of discrimination in the workplace. The current president has
loaded the Labor Relations Board with anti-Labor
activists, who routinely block union organizing.

The current president rode to power on the wings of the transformed remnants of the old racists. In his first campaign for high office, the younger Mr. Bush embraced the president of Bob Jones University, a school which openly opposes inter-racial marriage. The right-wing Christian base of the contemporary Republican party comes directly from the segregationists of the sixties.

Jerry Falwell, head of the Moral Majority, got his start in public life by running a segregated Christian school. During the bitter fights of 1956–64 to desegregate schools, some states, like Alabama, Virginia, and Louisiana, closed all public schools rather than integrate them. Then some bright spirits, including Falwell, got the idea of opening all-white schools that would pretend to be something else, namely, "Christian academies."

The old hates that poured into streets from Chicago to Birmingham have eased, in some cases even disappeared, but in parts of the country they have only taken new names, forming a new nexus of hatred—anti-gay, anti-woman, and ferociously nativist.

In the sixties and early seventies, when we encountered this kind of hatred, we would take to the streets and organize for change. Today, I see few signs that anyone wants to organize for change. I don't know if people feel so overwhelmed by the war in Iraq, the threat of terrorism, the damage to the environment, the destruction of women's rights, the loss of jobs, the long decline in real wages, along with the gutting of federal anti-poverty programs, that we don't know where or how to start. I don't know if people are in narcissistic cocoons of cell phones and iPods that make us oblivious to the world outside.

We've survived worse, my friend the novelist Valerie Wilson Wesley says, and she's right: we survived slavery, we survived Dred Scott and the Taney Court, lynch mobs, back-alley abortions, no suffrage for women, poll taxes, and the McCarthy-HUAC hysteria. We can surely survive the Alito court, the Ashcroft-Gonzalez Justice Department and all their attendant ills.

I am tired, V I is tired, but we both need to get back on our horses and try to raise the siege of Orleans.

Notes

1 Oddly enough, these are the same people who today make up the religious right-wing of the Republican party, and they spend every day trying to legislate their brand of sexual morality.
2 I will not use that ugly word, even in a quotation.
3 Quoted in Taylor Branch, *At Canaan's Edge*, Simon & Schuster, 2006, p. 511.
4 In 1976, I married a man I had met while working as a secretary at the University in the late sixties. He is a physicist, and a man whose amazing qualities of intellect, humor and empathy would require a separate essay to enumerate. When we married, he was a widower with three teenaged sons.
5 The city's central business district, named for the trains which form a mile square loop around it.
6 Quoted in Branch, *At Canaan's Edge*, pp. 232–3.
7 The newly elected Democratic Congress has voted to increase the minimum wage, for the first time in a decade. As I write in January 2007, Mr. Bush is threatening to veto this bill.

3

Not Angel, Not Monster, Just Human

When my room-mate hadn't returned by eleven, I started calling area hospitals. I finally found her at New York Presbyterian, the hospital attached to Columbia University. Weak from hemorrhaging, she had collapsed on a sidewalk a few blocks from our apartment; some good Samaritan had called for an ambulance.

It was June of 1970. New York, where I was working as a secretary, had passed a law legalizing abortion, but it wouldn't take effect for another six weeks. My pregnant room-mate couldn't wait another six weeks. The married politician who had impregnated her was abandoning her and she didn't have the resources, either financial or emotional, to take on a pregnancy and a baby.

I offered to go with her to the coat-hanger abortionist she found, but we weren't friends—I was a stranger who had answered her ad for a room-mate. She preferred to go alone, and she was alone when she almost died.

I had gone to New York that summer, hoping to get a job in the world of writing. I didn't have a fantasy of finding a garret and writing some amazing novel, because in New York even a garret, even in 1970, took serious income to support. Nor could I imagine writing a novel. I knew I was quick with words and could write well enough for other people to like what I said, but in the milieu where I'd grown up, novels belonged to people who were smarter, more interesting, more creative—and more masculine–than me.

My ignorance of the writing world was profound. I thought I could show the *New Yorker*, or *New York*, or *Harper's*, or the dailies, or any of the thousand magazines and papers published there, examples of my unpublished history essays and short stories—what a portfolio!—and they might take me on in some very junior capacity. I didn't realize then that good journalism was as demanding as good fiction—I just thought, fast turnaround, clever phrases, I can do that.

Armed with $200 scraped together from odd jobs and borrowed from a friend, I made the rounds but never got past the front desk. I had no contacts. I was so ignorant I didn't know you needed a sponsor to get into one of those places. And even if I'd known, I wouldn't have been able to figure out how to find one. It's possible, too, that my skills are not now and weren't then, best suited for journalism, but I never got far enough in the process to have them evaluated. The only publication that would even talk to me was *Time*, and they wanted me to be a typist in their accounting department.

When I was twenty-three, you could live for a couple of weeks on $200 in New York. But as my short grace period drew to a close and I began to panic about what I might live on, I fulfilled my destiny and became a secretary. It was through my workplace that I found my room-mate.

Our paths diverged a few weeks after she left the hospital; I don't even remember her name after all these years. She entered Columbia's school of journalism and moved into campus housing. I found new room-mates and continued my job as a secretary.

However, when I returned to Chicago that fall, I became active in reproductive politics. I trained with the Rev. E. Spencer Parsons, head of the Clergy Consultation Service on Problem Pregnancies, and became an active part of the women's liberation movement.

On my return to the Midwest, I returned as well to the dissertation I was writing on the nineteenth-century roots of American Christian fundamentalism.[1] To support myself, I took a job with a small firm that held conferences on how to implement President Nixon's executive orders on affirmative action. And in my spare time, I read crime fiction.

My mother had been a great reader of mysteries. In my teens I started on the ones she brought home from the library, including Dorothy Salisbury Davis—who, to my amazement and delight, has become my mentor and good friend all these years later—and Rex Stout, creator of Nero Wolf. Stout grew up in the 1890s in the same part of Kansas as I did, attending a one-room school about eight miles from my own alma mater, Kaw Valley District 95. (When I was on the baseball team, Stout's old school, Wakarusa District Six, always clobbered Kaw Valley.)

All during January, 1971, when I was supposed to be reading Knappen on Puritanism, and Woodward and Franklin on slavery and Reconstruction, I sat in the university library stacks reading Allingham, Lathen, and Blake on murder. A fellow student discovered me at my secret vice and told me to read Chandler.

I started with *The Big Sleep*, the first Chandler novel, and read through *The Long Goodbye*, taking in his short stories along the way. My favorite Chandler remains his short story, "The Red Wind." It was through Chandler that I met the staple of noir fiction, the sexually—very—active woman who is the cause of all that goes wrong in the world around her.

The first of these femmes fatales is Carmen Sternwood in *The Big Sleep*. Ms. Sternwood's initial appearance comes when she meets Philip Marlowe in the foyer of her father's mansion. She greets him as every woman I've ever known greets a strange man:

> [S]he turned her body slowly and lithely, without lifting her feet. Her hands dropped limp at her sides. She tilted herself towards me on her toes. She fell straight back into my arms. I had to catch her or let her

crack her head on the tessellated floor. I caught her under her arms and she went rubber-legged on me instantly. I had to hold her close to hold her up. When her head was against my chest she screwed it around and giggled at me.

If you are actually able to perform this manoeuver, you will find a good job as a circus contortionist—I always get lost between tilting forward on my toes and falling straight back.

At the end of this complicated novel—filled with so many murders that Chandler famously couldn't account for one of the bodies during the film adaptation—it turns out that while Carmen was certainly a murderer, most of the murders in the book were committed by men whom she'd driven past the point of reason by her sexuality.

I spent a lot of time that winter thinking about Carmen, and thinking about my New York roommate's near-death experience. Yes, *The Big Sleep* is a novel, it is fiction. So is the widely-hailed *Miracle Game* by Czech dissident Josef Skvorecky, in which the corruption in the Czech government and the crushing of the 1968 Prague spring were both caused by the duplicity of a highly-sexed female student who worked for the secret police, had sex with her professors and colleagues, and then betrayed them all to the Secret Police. So also is the story of Eve, who uses her brand-new, never-road-tested sexual powers to get Adam to eat the apple. All these fictions, created by men, were meant to define me and to box me off the pages and into the margins of life.

I began to understand that winter that I was being told over and over, by many books, most movies, much advertising, by history, my family, even, indirectly, by the University of Chicago history faculty, that I existed only in the body; that it was my fundamental nature to use my body to try to get good boys to do bad things; that if I succeeded, then I would get pregnant, which was my just punishment for existing in the body; if I chose to terminate the pregnancy, I should die, because I was avoiding the justice due me. In film and fiction in that era, if a young woman had an abortion, she had to die, as was the case in a heart-wrenching episode of Ben Gazzara's *Run for Your Life*: the girl dies in Gazzara's arms, if I remember correctly, and then he metes out justice to the cold-hearted, fiendish doctor who performed the abortion.

When I started my doctoral work, the head of the European field committee told entering students that women could memorize and parrot things back, but that we weren't capable of producing original work. In his history of Western civilization, he included no accomplishments by women.[2]

Thirteen women started the US history program with me in the fall of 1968. I was the only one who returned our second year, and that wasn't because I was a better scholar, or smarter—it was because the other twelve women all figured out other things to do with their time instead of enduring the department's relentless misogyny. I was simply too confused and depressed to work out an alternate career. Besides, I was trying to prove to my father that I was as smart as my brothers.

Second-wave feminism began to come into its own as a movement in the early seventies; other women were thinking about these issues and articulating some of the cultural norms and pressures and definitions placed on women. Robin Morgan, Ti-Grace Atkinson, Gloria Steinem, all spoke to different aspects of power, powerlessness, of being what Simone de Beauvoir had labeled "the Other." And they spoke to me.

Chandler's Carmen Sternwood didn't make me believe in women's rights—I had been dabbling in those waters since I was nineteen and chaired the first commission on the status of women at the University of Kansas. In August, 1970, while I was working in New York, I took part in the historic strike and March for Women's Equality down Fifth Avenue. It was an exhilarating, liberating afternoon, but one image that abides is passing a men's club and seeing the men staring at us from a third-floor window; they were red-faced with drink and they were laughing down at us.

I had been a believer in equality, but in the winter of 1971, I became a feminist. I became angry at my powerlessness—my personal powerlessness, in my patriarchal family, and my patriarchal history department—and the powerlessness that society bestowed on all women.

That winter I said no, no to being defined by my sexuality, no to having my body controlled by the government, the church, or other avatars of male power, no to endless harassment on the job—men following me down the hall whistling and saying, "Looking good, slick," was a small harassment, compared to dead rats and used tampons in their lockers that women breaking into the trades still encounter today—or in the classroom (one friend recounted her first day of class at Washington University in St. Louis; the instructor asked all the women in class to cross their legs. When they did so, puzzled, he said, "Good: now that the gates to hell are shut, we can proceed").

The seventies were years of brave women taking risks. Southern senators had added discrimination against women to the Civil Rights Act of 1964, in the hopes of so ridiculing the bill that Congress would vote it down. In fact, the language used by the men who introduced Title VII, the section which specifically outlaws discrimination against women, was riddled with bawdy innuendoes and tired old jokes about women. This so enraged the women in Congress that even those who had been opposed to the Civil Rights Act broke party and ideological ranks to vote it into law.

Under Representative Martha Griffiths' passionate leadership, the bill took on teeth for women. They began redressing a long litany of ills: suing AT&T for denying them access to the better-paying technical and engineering jobs; sitting in at magazine offices to demand fairer coverage and access to better jobs; organizing for access to contraception; organizing for the right to borrow money in their own names; organizing to end laws that kept pregnant women out of the workplace; trying to close the gap in women's pay.

In the 1830s, American women earned roughly 12 cents on the male dollar. By 1977, that had climbed to $59\frac{1}{2}$ cents—a gain of a penny every three years. The closest we've ever come was in 2000, when we made it to 79 cents for every dollar men earn, but in recent years, we've lost ground.[3]

These gains didn't come easily. It took a lot of lawsuits, a lot of organizing, and a lot of courage. The four women who began the successful class-action suit against AT&T were fired for bringing suit, and were not able to find work for many years afterwards. Almost everyone trying to better women's estate faced serious harassment.

The first speak-outs on rape were held in 1971. In my youth, we were often told that "If rape is inevitable, relax and enjoy it"; this slogan was used commonly to suggest ways of dealing with any inevitable, slightly disagreeable situation, but the implication was that women secretly desired violation.

A common, and successful, defense in rape trials was to argue that women had rape fantasies, and that

modern psychiatry proved that these meant that women
wished to be raped: women put themselves in the path
of rapists to get their fantasies fulfilled. For many
women, this attitude made it hard to distinguish among
their fears, their desires, and what was being imposed
on them. In the seventies, women began organizing
rape crisis centers and domestic violence centers to help
each other with these most difficult problems.

As for me, I wanted to write a crime novel. I wanted
to create a woman who would turn the tables on the
dominant views of women in fiction and in society. The
more I read, the more I realized that a woman's moral
character was determined by her sexuality: if she were
chaste, she was good, but helpless, unable to act. If she
had sex, she could act, but she could perform only evil
deeds.

In British crime fiction, a widow or a divorcee
signaled sexual availability to both the reader and
the other characters. She might not be the main villain,
but she would inevitably be duplicitous. Women could
be vamps, or virgins, or, very often, victims, but they
couldn't be effective problem solvers.[4] In short, women
could be Coventry Patmore's "Angel in the House,"[5]
or they could be monsters, but they couldn't be human.

I read and thought a great deal during the seventies,
but I was still living in a world of daydreams. I could
imagine myself with a finished book in print, but I
couldn't imagine myself actually writing it.

During that decade, I scribbled a few pages about a

very tough private eye named Minerva Daniels, a chain-smoking, rotgut-drinking loner, into whose life came a slim-hipped, broad-shouldered man with an assumed name, who would turn out to be the main villain. Minerva didn't go very far; parody takes a lot of work and a different kind of sensibility than mine. I needed a character who was more grounded in the world of the real. And I needed more confidence than I could get from consciousness-raising groups.

It wasn't until I was in my early thirties, working as a manager for CNA Insurance, that I finally sat down to turn the stories I told in my head into a novel. When I began writing my first book, *Indemnity Only*, I was trying to create a woman who was a person, not an angel or a monster. But I wasn't thinking of what it means to be a woman hero in a positive way. I knew what I *didn't* want my detective to be, but not what she *should* be. As a result, I put her into the mainstream of the hard-boiled form—orphaned, with a Smith & Wesson, drinking whisky—instead of thinking about what special role a woman detective might play.

The one aspect of my detective I thought about consciously from the start was her sexuality and the role of sex in my stories. Serial killers who torture women and children, or rapists who prey on women and children, play an enormous—and enormously titillating, not to mention enormously lucrative—role in today's fiction. I vowed not to use sex to exploit my characters—or readers. I also wanted my hero, V I to be a sexual being and a moral person at the same time. Too often the unmarried career woman in the modern mystery has depraved sexual appetites and has to die—as was true of Carolyn Polhemus in *Presumed Innocent* or Alix Forrest in *Fatal Attraction.* In other cases, she may not be depraved but her appetites take a lot of satiation.

V I's emotional involvements do sometimes cloud her judgments. That is a fact of life for men and women both. V I has lovers, but her sexuality does not prohibit her from making clear moral decisions and acting on them. V I isn't flawless. Merely, she is an adult, with the same freedoms that men have to act, to move, to make decisions, to fall in love, experience sex, even to be wrong, without any of those things making her a monster.

On January 22, 1973, the United States Supreme Court decided in *Roe v. Wade* that "the right of the individual . . . to be free from unwarranted governmental intrusion into matters so fundamentally affecting a person as the decision whether to bear or beget a child" was protected by the 14th Amendment to the Constitution.[6] For a space of about thirty seconds, women all over America had the right to be full adults. They were not accountable to their fathers, or to surrogate fathers in the guise of lovers, courts, churches, for how they made the most vital decision any human faces: when or whether to become a parent.

Although the women's movement continued to address very serious issues of economic equity, child care, poverty, and welfare for the next three decades, the cornerstone of recognizing that women are adults is to recognize our right to control our fertility.

For most of recorded history, going well back into ancient Sumer, women have been property, first of our fathers, then of our husbands or brothers. The most important aspect of owning women was the ownership, or control, of their sexuality. Controlling female sexuality gave men effectual control over women's fertility. It subordinated women to the demands of maternity. It made women sexually available on demand to their partners. This dominance gained a theological underpinning by demonizing female sexuality: women had to be controlled—otherwise our sexual impulses would destroy men, just as Eve had done to Adam.

The idea that women might control their bodies, that they might not be willing to accept pregnancy as a "punishment" for sex, was so offensive to some people that they began mobilizing to overturn *Roe* and outlaw both abortion and contraception even before the Court's decision was announced. In the seventies, I served on the board of the National Abortion Rights Action League in Illinois. Anti-abortion fanatics picketed our meetings.

They began attacking clinics, murdering doctors, assaulting nurses and patients. They entered a Cleveland clinic, poured gasoline on a nurse and set fire to

her, severely injuring her and terrifying patients
prepped and awaiting surgery. They assassinated doctors in Buffalo, Vancouver and Pensacola and shot
another doctor in Kansas. In all, almost six thousand
acts of terror have been committed against clinics and
their staff since *Roe* was issued. This does not include
the hundreds of thousands of acts against patients,
which include phone calls in the middle of the night,
filled with nauseating filth; stalking abortion recipients;
sending them hate mail, and other acts.

Hand-in-hand with this hate goes a twisted idea about
women, sex, and pregnancy. I don't know how many
times I have heard an anti-abortion activist say that
women who die from illegal abortions "get what's
coming to them."

When I took part in the March for Women's Lives in
April, 2004, a handful of anti-abortion zealots turned
out to try to harass the 1.1 million women and men
marching in Washington. They carried signs that said,
"Jezebels, you are bound for hell," and "Get back to
the bedroom and the kitchen where you belong." One
even celebrated the murders of three doctors, including
Dr. Barnett Slepian, saying, "Kopp Popped, Barnett
Dropped, Hallelujah." Fox, CNN, and the *New York
Times* all gave more coverage to these three hundred
protestors than they did to the march itself, but none of
these media included pictures of the antis' hate-filled
posters.

With the aggressive support first of Ronald Reagan

and the senior Bush, and now the junior Bush and their extremist appointees, the FBI and the federal judiciary have either ignored these threats, or actively supported the terrorists. In 1995 a Reagan appointee in New York, Judge John Sprizzo, refused to uphold convictions against two men arrested for blockading a clinic because they had acted out of religious conviction. After four years of expensive appeals, the clinic finally got the Supreme Court to overturn Sprizzo's ruling. In the meantime, those two men were free to continue acts of terror against other clinics. Many other clinics also have to fight terrorists on their own, without government support, one battle at a time.

Reagan and the two Bushes have come out every January 22 to address the antis. Despite strong evidence presented by clinics and women's groups, they have refused to allow the FBI or the AFT to investigate this national network of terror. At every international population conference, Reagan and both Bushes have joined with Islamic fundamentalists and the Vatican to oppose women's access to contraception and abortion. The self-anointed leader of the free world comes from the *only* developed country to side with religious zealots against women's freedom.[7]

This campaign of terror has been very effective. Most American abortion providers have quit. The procedure has been outlawed or banished in all but thirteen percent of American counties. Fewer than ten percent of medical schools train students in how to perform

surgical abortions. In America we are close to the point
of having a legal right to a non-existent medical procedure. Because poor women and minors have the least
power in society, the US Congress acted early through
the notorious Hyde Amendment to deny poor women
public aid funds for abortion: only a handful of states
now fund abortions for women on Medicaid (New York
does, but Illinois, where I live, does not). Most states
also restrict the access of minors to abortion, but they
do not pay attention to male sexual behavior.

When I did clinic escort duty in Chicago, the antis
kicked us, spat on us and called us Christ killers
("Christ killers, baby killers," they would chant). They
did all these things, as their ringleader told me—
shortly before he ran his car over a security guard—
" to make sure these girls have help in living their lives
right." This person was a Catholic seminarian, himself
so young he wasn't yet shaving, but he did not see
women going into a clinic: he saw girls.

A girl is a child. Most cultures, in most times, have
viewed women not as full, legal adults but as a cross
between children and chattel animals. This view so
pervades American culture that many educated, otherwise empathic people cannot understand why women
object to being called girls. If women were indeed
regarded as full adults, equal to men, there would be
no argument about pay equity.

Girls, children, are not sophisticated enough to make
difficult moral choices unless they are told how. Many

religious groups continue today to preach women's
God-ordained second-class status. Southern Baptists,
one of America's largest denominations, declared in
1984 that since Eve initiated sin in the Garden of Eden,
women should forever be subject to men. The denomination began then to cut off funds from member
congregations where women preached or served as
deacons. Today this denomination has retreated behind
the walls of a rigid fundamentalism, running Christian
academies for their children, colleges for their young
adults, political day camps for their young activists, but
making certain that at all times they are sheltered from
any opinions that contradict their view of men, women,
God, and the world.

One of the books at Liberty Baptist Church, the Rev.
Jerry Falwell's Virginia congregation, shows an organization chart that depicts human relations with God:
From God at the top the lines of authority descend to
the local church, then to the father, who in turn is in
charge of the mother and children. The chart is called
"God's chain of command."

The religious right sees harm from all the gains
women have made since 1970, but the full heat of their
fury against women has burned against reproductive
rights. Swollen with their successes in fighting abortion, these women haters are now campaigning against
contraception. A quarter of the states already have laws
permitting pharmacists to refuse to fill prescriptions
for contraceptives; some twenty others are considering

such laws. John Kerry himself felt compelled to sign on
to this legislation when it was proposed at the national
level, in the name of "freedom of religion."

We are in a peculiar state of mind in America these
days. We want untrammeled capital markets. We think
speed limits, handgun controls and taxes are an unwarranted intrusion into personal liberty. But we feel
an overwhelming need to control women's sexuality.

The junior Bush has given free rein to corporate
veniality, to the proliferation of automatic weapons on
our streets, and to the death of over half a million
people in Iraq, but he is adamant about controlling the
sexual behavior of women both at home and abroad. He
does this, he says, in the name of promoting "a culture
of life." He desperately needs doctors to serve in Iraq,
but no one who supports abortion rights can go. He
won't allow family planning aid to go to countries where
health care providers either counsel or perform abortions. And his home state of Texas was the first in the
nation to allow pharmacists to opt out of filling birth
control prescriptions. Little girls, you must get Daddy's
permission for what you want to do in the privacy of
your bedrooms.

The ferocity of the right-wing's attack on women is
proof of the success of second-wave feminism. Many
positive changes have taken place in the last thirty
years, not just in women's estate, but in relations
between men and women. It's not just that women
are now occupying high office, even if their ride to

office and tenure there is proving bumpy. It's not just that women don't need a male co-signer for loans.

There's been a sea-change in the way many men and women are relating to each other. I see it in many young couples I know, where they discuss all aspects of their lives, and where everyone's happiness has to be considered in reaching a decision on work, relocating, having children, doing chores. I see these changes reflected in many of the mysteries I read, where men are writing about women who are friends or colleagues, not just victims, vamps or villains.

As women's real-world horizons have expanded, so have they in fiction. Today we have a legion of active women protagonists, not just my own V I Warshawski and Marcia Muller's Sharon McCone, but Val McDermid's many unusual heroines, Nevada Barr's Anna Pigeon, Kay Scarpetta, and a host of others. Fifteen years ago I knew all of the women writing books with strong women heroes. Today there are so many I can't keep track of them.

The reaction to women's increased power to speak varies greatly. On the positive side, we have received a substantial embrace of welcome, from readers of both sexes as well as from publishers. Our growing numbers in the crime fiction field tell the story: in 1986, when I started the organization Sisters in Crime, women published about a third of American crime novels. Today we make up almost fifty percent of active US crime writers.

Sisters in Crime itself came out of the sense that many women writers had of being second-class citizens in the crime writing world. Many of us encountered both fans and writers at crime conferences who assumed we wrote as a hobby, not as a serious vocation.

Other issues affected our careers in more substantive ways. These had to do with lack of reviews of books by women and the much shorter length of time our books stayed in print and on the shelves. When Sisters started the Book Review Project we found that—adjusting for the fact that men published more titles—books by men were reviewed seven times as often as books by women (this refers only to crime fiction). We found that books by women writers stayed in print on average for a third the length of time that books by men did. These facts severely affected women's ability to earn a living as writers.

Like other women trying to organize for change, our path wasn't free of obstacles. Women were told their publishing contracts would be canceled if they joined. When I proposed a study of why so much film and fiction revolved around sadistic acts, I was pilloried in the fanzines and accused of promoting censorship. In other words, degrading women in print and film was protected by the First Amendment, but questioning the degradation was not. The members of Sisters in Crime were so worried by these attacks that they voted to shelve any effort at studying graphic sadism.

This sadism has been a growth industry. Despite the

many welcome changes of the last twenty years, we are bombarded with books, movies, songs, and above all, video games, which show women being violated in horrific ways. These run the gamut from mainstream films where women's chief role is as prostitute—witness the successful re-release of Sharon Stone's *Basic Instinct* in 2006, which includes what some reviewers call "the classic film moment of Sharon Stone's spread-leg interrogation"—to video games where players can rape, maim, and kill misbehaving prostitutes.

Like the prostitute who cheers up Clark Gable in *Gone with the Wind*, in fiction and film, the woman who understands that she really *is* a prostitute is a contented animal, happy to be able to have this kind of easy camaraderie with men through her body. The same woman appears in contemporary film or fiction—as Robert Parker's widely-praised hooker-in-distress, April Kyle demonstrates.

These depictions are very remote from reality: most American sex workers were sexually abused as children, and become prostitutes because they were conditioned as children to believe that they existed only in the body and only to respond to male sexual needs. There are no completely accurate data on how many children in America are sexually abused; studies of sexual violence against girls show a range of from one in four to one in eight; for boys the figure is about one in ten. Even the most conservative estimates show a staggering amount of violence against children. Sexual assault against children causes long-term, irremediable damage, and to glamorize it by showing prostitutes as doing it for fun only deepens the problem.

Women of all ages are at high risk of rape in America: it happens to about one in six of us. Focusing on the damage this kind of violence does to women gets feminists like me blamed for creating what the *Wall Street Journal* calls "a culture of rape"—an op-ed theme they revisit more-or-less annually, going back to 1991.

Nonetheless, the threat of rape is a potent one, a threat that is intended to scare women into silence. Rex Stout, a champion of civil liberties, made the point quite clearly in his last Nero Wolfe book, *A Family Affair*, published in 1975. One of the characters is a feminist. She is strident, hostile and humorless, a "man hater," as feminists are often portrayed in fiction. Archie Goodwin, Wolfe's sidekick, advises fellow de- tective Saul Panzer to rape her in order to get her to co- operate in an interrogation. Archie is saying that as a feminist, the woman is speaking out of turn—in this case, she is keeping silent out of turn: she is refusing to speak when Archie and Saul command her to. She is out of control and must be punished. No one is further out of control than an admitted feminist. Rape is the necessary means to subdue her.

As women's speech began taking up more room, fiction and film no longer told us that we *ought* to be raped. Rather, they began demonstrating the rape, and showing the ensuing humiliation which forces women out of public life. In Heywood Gould's *Double Bang*, for instance, the alleged heroine is a psychoanalyst in New York City. In the words of Michael Korda, the president of Simon and Schuster who sent me bound galleys of the book in hopes I would give it a jacket blurb:

> At the novel's center is Karen Winterman—a beautiful psychoanalyst who falls for a seductive psychopath who just happens to be a drug addict and her new patient. Breaking the cardinal rule of her profession, she finds herself, in the wake of her lover's murder, trapped in a series of ever more compromising positions: homicide suspect, hitman's target, key witness, chief mourner, unwitting victim . . . [The book also] brings new meaning to the phrase "police brutality."

At the book's end the psychoanalyst has been so damaged by her beguiling patient that she gives up her professional practice and returns to her parents' Pennsylvania farm. She has learned her lesson. She has shut up and retreated from being a woman, working on her own in the big city, to being a girl—a child—back under the protection of her parents.

As I worked on this essay in the fall of 2006, a gunman invaded an Amish school in Pennsylvania, sent the boys home, sexually abused the girls and then murdered five of them.

Writing on this in the *New York Times*, Bob Herbert said:

> Imagine if a gunman had gone into a school, separated the kids on the basis of race or religion and then shot only the black kids. Or only the white kids. Or only the Jews. There would have been thunderous outrage . . . and the attack would have been seen for what it really was: a hate crime. None of that occurred because these were just girls, and we have become so accustomed to living in a society saturated with misogyny that violence against females is . . . expected.[8]

I could continue a litany of sadistic treatment of women for many pages. Here are just a few: the big four television networks—CBS, ABC, NBC and Fox are currently running an ad from a major credit card company that shows a man swiping his card's magnetic stripe through a woman's buttocks, while a phone company ad shows three naked women holding a phone bill, with the tagline, "When was the last time you got screwed."

In the meantime, the big four refuse ads for contraceptives. Although some cable channels directed at women will now advertise birth control, the major companies have been cowed by threats of boycotts by anti-reproductive-rights zealots.

The United States is the only developed country where it is difficult, if not downright impossible, to discuss sex and fertility. The government, to the tune of

200 million dollars a year, sponsors "abstinence-only" programs in the nation's schools. These programs often tell outright lies about contraceptives, claiming that they only work half the time, that they cause cancer, that condoms and other barrier methods don't stop sexually transmitted diseases. The government repeatedly posts false or misleading information about contraception and the side-effects of abortion on the website for the Centers for Disease Control.

We have reached a point where a woman's body is not only an object—billboards outside most airports in America show graphic imagery of large-breasted women, major networks carry pornographic advertising, movies, novels, and video games reify women—but we utterly divorce the female body from issues of fertility, pregnancy, breast-feeding, or contraception. Those topics are taboo. It's as if we want to force women to be the monsters of demonic sexuality that western mythology has labeled them, and then punish them if they aren't chaste, or if they refuse pregnancy.

As women are bombarded with images of themselves as sexual objects or sexual monsters, as the threat of rape hovers in the background of fiction as well as life, women seem to seek to appear harmless. For instance, young women entering Northwestern University's medical school asked a woman professor to call them "girls," instead of "women"—they said the word "woman" sounded too harsh, too confrontational to them.

Another side effect is that successful women try to disappear physically. We read a lot about the obesity epidemic in America, but for women in public life, the goal is to become ever thinner. If women are occupying powerful public space, they try to make themselves physically invisible. Carly Fiorina in the boardroom, Katie Couric on the evening news, Condoleezza Rice in the State Department—all these women are thin, some so thin it's painful to look at them. It's as if they are saying, "Don't hurt us, we're really still the tiny little girls you need us to be."[9]

When I read contemporary crime fiction, over and over I see the heroine described as weighing 118 pounds, although her height is usually five foot six or taller. These heroines are called "big," in books by men and women both. You can count the ribs on a five-and-a-half-foot tall woman who weighs 118 pounds. She isn't big, she's small, and she shouldn't be out on those streets tackling thugs. No matter how skilled she is at karate, she has a serious weight disadvantage.[10]

Women as constructors of fiction—women as shapers of experience—are relatively new in western literature. In the early seventeenth century, the governor of Massachusetts Bay condemned his neighbor, the poet Anne Hopkins. She had lost her reason, he said, "by occasion of giving herself wholly to reading and writing, and had written many books." He added that "if she had attended her household affairs, and such things as belong to women . . . she had kept her wits."

It has taken the hard work of many women standing up to excoriation—or in the case of writers like Kate Chopin dying in the face of it—to come to our present situation, where women have easy access to books, both as readers and as writers.

But as women's speech has increased—as women have begun taking up more space—we have struck at the heart of a complicated sense of power. Because male speech historically defined the female, we are grasping something fundamental when we say we will define ourselves.

Anti-abortion zealots condemn women who control their own fertility for "playing God" with their bodies. In speech and in action, when we say we will define ourselves, the roadblocks put up by religion, government, boards of directors, become formidable.

Some years ago, the screen- and crime writer Roger Simon called to ask me to join his new organization, the International Crime Writers Association. He described a management team of some twenty international writers, all men. I said I wasn't comfortable lending my name to such a male-dominated group. Roger said, "Are you still doing feminism? I've already done that."

Feminism was a fad, it had its moment, it's gone, let's do gangster rap now. But I'm still doing feminism. And so is my detective, V I Warshawski. We are both dogged, even if we can't keep up with modern fashions.

A few years ago a group of women came to one of my readings in Chicago. They introduced themselves to me afterwards as wives of out of work steelworkers. With the death of the mills on Chicago's south side, some of their husbands had been out of work for ten years; these women worked two jobs to keep food on the table and a roof overhead. They told me they had not read a book since leaving high school until someone told them V I grew up in their neighborhood. They came to my lecture to tell me that the blue-collar girl detective helped them get through this very difficult hand that life had dealt them.

So although my words are only water squeezed from a rock, and although there are many days where I feel as though my voice, my very self were being crushed beneath that rock, these women have told me to get up, sit down, and keep writing.

Notes

1 I ultimately got my PhD in 1977. Barbara Pym, in *Less than Angels*, Plume 1990, calls someone's dissertation an elderly infirm relative who needs constant care—the best description I've ever seen.

2 The first edition of the *Rise of the West* attributed early agriculture to women, but that contribution had dropped out by the time I was in graduate school.

3 On average today, American women earn 76 cents on the male dollar; in the highly paid technology sector, the amount rises to a dizzying 82 cents. This figure is an average of all pay for all full-time workers of any race and any job. Cf. www.equalpay.info.

4 There were some exceptions, most notably Nicholas Blake's Georgia Strangeways, who is both feminine and effective as the central character in *The Smiler with the Knife*.

5 See Chapter 1 for a detailed discussion of the angel.

6 *Roe* was issued in tandem with *Doe v. Bolton*, a case where the mother is in danger or had been raped, or the fetus had significant abnormalities/defects. Neither *Roe* nor *Doe* allowed "abortion on demand" as the religious right has claimed; both cases allowed a significant state interest in pregnancy, and Justice Blackmun specifically allowed doctors to act as moral agents on behalf of women.

7 Countries with the most restrictive abortion laws also have the highest abortion rates according to the head of the UN Population Division. Cf also Gloria Feldt, *The War on Choice*, Bantam 2005, p. 71. President Clinton supported reproductive rights during his eight years in the White House, but the younger Bush has gone even further than his father and Reagan in opposing access not just to abortion and contraception—under his direction, Federal agencies promulgate lies about such things as the use of condoms to prevent STD's, the efficacy of contraception, and the psychological effects of premarital sex.

8 Bob Herbert, "Why Aren't We Shocked," *New York Times*, October 16, 2006.

9 In her memoir, *Tough Choices*, Fiorina describes having to go to strip joints to be "on the team" in her days as a junior exec.

10 African-American writers like Valerie Wilson Wesley and BarbaraNeely offer a welcome antidote to the obsession with boniness in contemporary heroines. V I Warshawski is 5'8" and weighs around 140–145 pounds.

4

The iPod and Sam Spade

In the summer of 1635, Governor John Winthrop signed a law empowering Massachusetts Bay magistrates to exile dissenters who posed a threat to public welfare. On October 9, 1635, this law was applied for the first time: Winthrop banished Roger Williams from the colony. Before the magistrates could deport him back to England, Williams fled down the coast to what is modern-day Rhode Island.

Roger Williams is heralded today as the father of religious liberty, a man who undertook the rigors of a New England winter alone—except for his long-suffering wife—in defense of his beliefs. That ardent Puritan might be astounded by such a paternity claim. Williams' quarrel with Massachusetts Bay was not that they were against religious liberty—which they were. His argument was that the Massachusetts churches were so impure that no godly man who was truly regenerate (as Williams knew himself to be) could pray with them. In fact, by 1635, Williams had come to the point where he could be certain only of his own and his wife's salvation, and would worship with no one else.

Everyone in Massachusetts Bay had to support the

colony's established Congregational church: regardless of their individual religious beliefs, whether Catholic, Jew, Quaker or Atheist, the law required them to attend Congregational services every Sunday, and to pay taxes to support the church.

However, only those who could prove they had experienced a saving conversion could be church members. And only male church members could vote for the magistrates who governed the colony.

A saving conversion, by the way, was a strenuous experience. It wasn't a Pat Roberson, Jerry Falwell, tears-on-TV routine. Puritans spent years in self-analysis, prayer, and spiritual torment before any ray of grace appeared. Church members interrogated prospective members for eight or more hours, even reading the diaries the candidates kept during the many years of their wrestling with doubt.[1]

Roger Williams agreed with the colony leaders, both about having to prove conversion to belong to the church, and the state's subordination to the church. He just didn't think Massachusetts Bay went far enough. To avoid legal prosecution from the Crown, New England Puritans claimed to be members of the Church of England; they were merely purifying it (hence Puritans).

In Williams' view, this was hair-splitting—either you separated from the Church of England, or you were part and parcel of all its episcopal and royal authority and corruption. Williams demanded that the Congregational churches in Massachusetts separate formally, as well as in practice. When they would not do so, Williams announced that the magistrates could not enforce the laws: only the saved, the elect were virtuous enough to obey laws in a fallen world.

Today, someone who believes as Williams did would probably live in Texas or Idaho, where he would have a little militia that drilled with assault weapons, and published pamphlets denouncing the government's terrorism against the individual. No one outside his camp would pay much attention to him, unless his eccentricity spilled over into confrontation with the law, as happened with David Koresh and the Branch Davidians in Waco, or Randy Weaver at Ruby Ridge.

In 1635, however, New England consisted of a thousand or so Europeans perched precariously on the edge of a vast wilderness. The Pequot Indians made hostile raids which erupted periodically into war. However much we may believe today that our English forebears stole their land, they did present a threat to European survival. In addition, until 1644, when the English Puritans took over Parliament, the Massachusetts colony charter was under constant threat of cancellation because of their disrespect for the Anglican church. With only rudimentary medicine, primitive agriculture and hostile original Americans, the colonists needed a strong sense of community to survive.

One man preaching to a thousand people that they

should not obey the law could destroy that community. In banishing Roger Williams, Governor Winthrop acted for the survival of the whole colony (as well, it must be admitted, as the survival of his own power within the colony). But who do our schoolbooks teach us to think is the hero of this drama? The man who preserved the colony? No. The hero is the man whose sense of individual conscience was so urgent that the survival of his fellow men, women and children became secondary to him.[2]

Winthrop and the other founders of Massachusetts Bay saw themselves as a community of the elect intended to serve as a "Modell of Christian Charity"[3] to the rest of the world. However, the Calvinism which dominated the minds of those who settled the northeast, and later migrated to the Midwest and West, placed its greatest emphasis on the individual. Whereas God judged ancient Israel as a nation, each New England man and woman was weighed on his or her own merits: God arbitrarily damned this one, saved that one. In such an atmosphere, individual, not community works, were what counted.

The sheer size of the new continent probably contributed to the prize placed on individualism: such a giant wilderness can make you feel small and alone. You need to assert yourself strenuously to make any impact on the vastness of the place.

Today, when much of America is pruned or paved, it's hard to imagine how terrifying the landscape must

have seemed to the English colonists who arrived in
Massachusetts Bay in 1630. The journals and histories
written by the Puritans focused chiefly on doctrinal
battles within their community, and with the Anglican
church at home. Occasionally they did write about what
Edward Johnson called "The Laborious Worke Christs
People Have in Planting this Wildernesse" in his 1654
history, *The Wonder-working Providence of Sion's
Saviour in New England.*

> Traveling through unknowne woods, and through
> watery scrampes [probably swamps], sometimes pas-
> sing through Thickets, where their hands are forced to
> make way for their bodies passage, and their feete
> clamber over the crossed Trees . . . [then sinking] into
> an uncertaine bottome in water . . . ragged Bushes
> scratch their legs fouly, even . . . to their bare skin in
> two or three hours . . . They rest them [on] the rocks
> where night takes them, their repast some small pit-
> tance of bread . . .

As soon as they had subdued this wilderness, Americans began to feel nostalgic for it, and to romanticize it.
Our earliest fictional hero was Natty Bumppo, the
intrepid frontiersman in Fennimore Cooper's Leather-
stocking novels. The place where Edward Johnson
scratched his legs fouly through his leggings to his
bare skin became a nurturing home to Bumppo.

"Your ways aren't my ways," Bumppo says to the

Englishwoman Elizabeth at the end of the first Leather-stocking novel.

> "I love the woods and ye relish the face of man. I eat when hungry and drink when adry [*sic*]; and ye keep stated hours and rules . . . I'm formed for the wilderness; if ye love me, let me go where my soul craves to be . . ."

Natty Bumppo may have been our first loner hero, but he quickly had many heirs. As the Great Plains became the new frontier of the mid-nineteenth century, the cowboy took over the role of frontiersman. Figures like Owen Wister's *The Virginian*, published to international acclaim in 1905, or even John Wayne or Clint Eastwood's screen personae, were famous because they were more at home in the saddle than in settled towns; the plains and mountains were where they knew how to survive. Natty once "travelled seventy miles alone with a rifle bullet in my thigh and then cut it out with my own jackknife." The man who could do that had to be a hero, not a fool: he set the standard for the American ideal of the individual.

About the same time that Cooper wrote his first Leatherstocking novel, Alexis de Tocqueville visited America. In *Democracy in America*, he frowned over the country's obsession with individualism. He considered it similar to selfishness: he wrote in 1840 that it disposes each member of the community to sever himself from the mass of his fellows and to draw apart with his family and friends, so that after he has thus formed a little circle of his own, he . . . leaves society at large to itself . . . [individualism] originates as much in deficiencies of mind as in perversity of heart.

De Tocqueville could not possibly make a dent on a trait so important to our national mythology. In her simple, beautifully written autobiography—which survives despite NBC's efforts to over-sentimentalize it—Laura Ingalls Wilder writes off-handedly about how self-sufficiency was an understood value in her world.

In 1881, the Ingalls family moved from their South Dakota farm into the nearby town for the winter. Everyone feared a hard winter, and Mrs. Ingalls wanted her daughters close enough to school to be able to attend throughout the snowy season. But the storms proved so harsh that trains could not get through with coal for five months; school was shut down. In fact, the blizzards were so severe that days would go by with the family completely cut off from the world around it. One morning Mr. Ingalls decided to go out into the blizzard to cross the street and check on his neighbors.

Laura stood at the window. She had cleared a peep-hole through the frost but she saw only blank white-ness. She could not see Pa at the door nor tell when he

left it. She slowly went back to the heater. Mary sat
silently rocking Grace. Laura and Carrie just sat.

"Now girls!" Ma said. "A storm outdoors is no
reason for gloom in the house."

"What good is it to be in town?" Laura said. "We're
just as much by ourselves as if there wasn't any town."

"I hope you don't expect to depend on anybody else,
Laura." Ma was shocked. "A body can't do that."

Ma is affirming the very point de Tocqueville condemned: the family drawn into its little circle, independent of society. And if, in fact, the Ingalls depended more
on the outside than they would like us to think—getting
their land from the government, their seed from the seed
company, cloth for their clothes from the dry goods
store, their farming implements from Sears, Roebuck or
John Deere—they did so much on their own—making
not only clothes but sheets and bedding, planting,
harvesting, eating little they did not grow—that we
can understand why they prized their self-reliance.

In America today, few claim or try to be so self-
sufficient. But we seem to prize the self-reliant ideal
more than ever. In fact, so much do we prize the
individual that we don't want to pay taxes to support
the common good. Issues about health care, libraries,
and schools are well known, but the "me and me only"
impulse goes deeper than that. In one hyper-wealthy
Silicon Valley town, where houses commonly sell for
more than two million dollars, the streets are full of

potholes: when I visited, I was told that people in the town would rather ruin their own cars than pay taxes so that someone else could drive in comfort.

The American dream is of a private home with a private yard, in which each child has their own room, their own iPod, their own computer and, by the time they're twelve or even younger, their own cell phones. We spend our waking moments plugged into our portable entertainment centers, our iPods, our Game Boys. We don't do our laundry in a community creek or Laundromat unless forced to by economic necessity; we all have our own washers or dryers.

We seem, in short, to withdraw as far as possible from each other, encased in our own worlds of sound. Even when people are sharing a table at a restaurant, or lovers are walking down the street entwined with each other, they aren't really present together: each is talking to someone else on their cell phones.

Americans aren't unique among the people of the earth in loving their cell phones and their cars, but they may be unusual in their abhorrence of public transportation, as well as the ways in which they turn their cars into an extension of their homes, private space where they can do as they please and no one can gainsay them.

When my mother was in the final stages of a difficult illness, I was often on the phone with my brother Jonathan, who lived with her during her last painful months. If I was driving, I would conscientiously pull over to the curb so that emotion wouldn't distract me from traffic and toss me into the path of another car. I mentioned this to my brother. He commuted twenty-six miles on the Interstate in a bus and said he saw the following things while looking down into people's cars:

People with newspapers spread open on the steering wheel.

People with books open on the steering wheel.

People putting on eye makeup or shaving while talking on the phone and steering with their knees.

People with iPods in their ears, not hearing cars honking.

People eating constantly, and almost anything, from chocolate bars to elaborate meals involving cutlery.

One particularly flexible man playing a tuba.

Alone in our little houses on wheels, we idealize the emotionally self-sufficient hero. He may need someone else to do his baking, grow his food, make his clothes, but he doesn't need emotional nurture to survive.

Early in *The Long Winter*, the Ingalls get a brief visit from a real individualist—Mr. Edwards, whose path has crossed theirs several times as they migrate around the country. He comes home with Mr. Ingalls for a fleeting visit on his way west. Laura remembers him as a

. . . tall, lean, lounging wildcat from Tennessee. The . . . lines in his leather-brown face were deeper, a knife scar was on his cheek that had not been there before, but his eyes were as laughing and lazy and keen as she remembered them.

"Oh, Mr. Edwards!" she cried out.

"You brought our presents from Santa Claus," Mary remembered.

"You swam the creek," Laura said. "And you went away down the Verdigris river . . ."

Mr. Edwards scraped his foot on the floor and bowed low. "Mrs. Ingalls and girls, I surely am glad to see you all again."

Mr. Edwards . . . said he was going on West with the train when it pulled out. Pa could not persuade him to stay longer . . .

"This here country, it's too settled-up for me. The politicians are a-swarming in already, and ma'am if'n there's any worst pest than grasshoppers it surely is politicians . . ."

Before Pa or Ma could speak, the train whistle blew loud and long. "There's the call," said Mr. Edwards, and got up from the table.

Mr. Edwards goes on to Oregon. As he leaves, he hides a twenty-dollar-bill in blind Mary's skirt, money to help her go to college.

Mr. Edwards is a loner who looks after himself. He doesn't marry and has no children. He deals with tough people—witness his knife scar—but remains chivalrous to true ladies, to children, and the disabled. A literary-minded person might describe him like this:

[D]own these mean streets a man must go who is not himself mean, who is neither tarnished nor afraid . . . He must be a complete man and a common man and yet an unusual man. He must be, to use a . . . weathered phrase, a man of honor—by instinct, by inevitability, without thought of it, and certainly without saying it . . . He will take no man's money dishonestly and no man's insolence without a due and dispassionate revenge . . .

The words, of course, are Raymond Chandler's, written sixty years ago to describe his detective hero, whom he thought of as a knight. He further says that his knight "is a lonely man and his pride is that you will treat him as a proud man or be . . . sorry you ever saw him."

English-bred Chandler was not creating a new kind of character in Philip Marlowe.[4] Instead, he was drawing on a long tradition, putting into words what Americans most prize in our heroes. Mr. Edwards is an almost mythical figure to the Ingalls girls—he appears only three times in their history, and each time it is as "the wildcat from Tennessee" who saves Christmas for them, or preserves their claim to their farm, or—in their final encounter—chivalrously helps blind Mary. He rides off into the West just like Shane. And, like Shane, or Philip Marlowe, he has no close human attachments, for people get in the way of heroism.

The loner hero has one other salient quality: he—and she—take justice into their own hands. Because they are working on the side of right against people who may be perverting the law, we trust their intuitive honor as being better than the law—just as Roger Williams trusted his own regenerate Christian sense of law more than he trusted the Massachusetts Bay magistrates.

When H.L. Mencken and George Jean Nathan founded *The Black Mask Quarterly* in 1920, they started a formal vehicle for bringing this loner hero to the American people. *The Black Mask* originally took westerns, horror stories, adventure and novelty stories as well as mysteries, but in 1926 new owners and editors made it an exclusive vehicle for mystery. It is the place where Dashiell Hammett and Raymond Chandler got their start as writers.

Another writer, Carroll John Daly wrote for the earliest issues of *The Black Mask*, creating in 1923 America's first hard-boiled detective, Race Williams, whose first name was chosen deliberately to evoke the human race. In one adventure Race Williams spelled out the private eye's character: "I'm sorry if I appear hard boiled or cold blooded . . . but them that live by the gun should die by the gun." But he did not believe in shooting people at whim: "I'm all for justice and fair play . . . My conscience is clear: I never bumped off a guy who didn't need it."

Race Williams also laid out the hard-boiled detective's attitude on justice and morality:

Right and wrong are not written on the statutes for me, nor do I find my code of morals in the essays of long-winded professors. My ethics are my own. I'm not saying they're good and I'm not admitting they're bad, and what's more I'm not interested in the opinions of others on that subject.

Carroll John Daly wrote that passage in 1923. It has an uncomfortable resonance with America's current posture toward the rest of the world.[5]

Race Williams was the supreme individualist, even down to defining his own morality; he killed lots of people, but only if they deserved it. At the outset of his writing career, Dashiell Hammett was even less concerned with ethics, even on such a personal level.

The Continental Op, the nameless detective about whom Hammett wrote many short stories for the *Black Mask*, and then his first full length novel, *Red Harvest*, has no ethics or morals. He is an individualist, pure and simple, whose only code is getting the job done and surviving.

Red Harvest is an appalling book, because the violence is so pervasive it infects even the detective: there is no one with whom the reader can empathize. The Continental Op solves the problems of Poisonville by pitting everyone involved in it against each other. He himself gets toked out of his mind on laudanum and alcohol and feels no remorse when he thinks he may have killed a woman in his drugged stupor.

With *The Maltese Falcon*, Hammett created a more attractive hero. Sam Spade, like the Continental Op—or Race Williams, or Mr. Edwards—takes justice into his own hands. Although he turns the criminals over to the police in the end, it is only after he has worked out everyone's role in the death of his partner and in the chase after the falcon.

Spade exhibits the trait which became the hallmark of all subsequent literary private investigators: the intuitive understanding of human motivations which make it possible to sort out a crime. He knows Brigid O'Shaughnessy must have killed his partner, not because of any hard forensic evidence, but because he knows his partner, understands his personality so well that Spade realizes only a beautiful woman could have lured Miles Archer into an alley and shot him at point-blank range.

Spade has a second characteristic which has also become common to the modern private eye—the ability to look at human motivations without flinching and without sentimentality. When Spade gets ready to "send Brigid O'Shaughnessy over," that is, to deliver her to the law, the scene is more physically wrenching for him than when the fat man slipped him a Mickey Finn and had Wilmer cosh him. But Spade deals with the fact that despite his attraction to her, Brigid is a villain. There is no room for a romanticized view of her: she is not going to repent and undergo a sentimental transformation.

Sam Spade made even more conquests outside *The Maltese Falcon* than he did on the page. "After reading *The Maltese Falcon*, I went mooning about in a daze of love such as I had not known for any character in literature since I encountered Sir Lancelot," Dorothy Parker wrote in the *New Yorker* in 1931, adding that she had read the book thirty or forty times in the two years since its publication.

The cynical journalist wasn't the only woman felled by Spade—or his creator: dozens went to bed with Dashiell Hammett when he moved from San Francisco to Los Angeles to join the throng trying to make money in Hollywood. Lillian Hellmann even left her husband in Los Angeles to follow Hammett to New York in 1931.

Hammett was one of the more complicated figures on the American literary scene.

Hammett grew up near Baltimore, in terrible poverty. In 1907, when he was thirteen, he had to leave school to help support his family. He joined the Pinkerton Agency in 1915, when he was twenty-one, but when America entered World War I, he joined the army as an ambulance driver, and in 1918 he contracted flu in the terrible epidemic that was sweeping through army camps. His lungs were damaged so severely that for years he often didn't have the strength to get out of bed. He lived on a very meager disability check and couldn't work consistently for any length of time. He briefly rejoined Pinkerton's, where he worked for only about four months before his lungs gave out on him.

His private life doesn't bear close inspection. He had a wife and two children whom he essentially abandoned when he moved to New York, rarely contributing to his daughters' or his wife's support, even though Spade had made him rich—at least briefly: Paramount put Hammett on a retainer at $2,000 a week—almost $27,000 a week in current dollars. Hammett threw the money away on his idea of the high life, including lavish parties that cost as much as $10,000 ($133,000 today) and long weekends of drinking with starlets and writers. Some of it went to settle a claim of forcible rape, which Hammett made no attempt to defend.

Despite his frail health, he was a prodigious drinker and smoker—he and Faulkner used to spend long weekends in Faulkner's New York apartment, ostensibly discussing literature, but in fact drinking so heavily that when they attended a dinner at the Knopfs in honor of Willa Cather, both men passed out (the servants were able to revive Faulkner and get him to the dining room, but Hammett they had to carry back down to the street and put into a taxi to his hotel.)

Despite his dubious private life, Hammett was Chandler's "man of honor" in public. He spent six months in a federal prison in 1951 when he refused to testify to Congress about the Civil Rights Congress, an organization on whose board he sat. The Congress provided bail for arrested labor organizers, many of whom were African-American, some of whom were Communists.

Since the days of the infamous Dies Committee of the 1930s, Congress and the FBI had closely identified Civil Rights activists with Communism. In the 1960s, when the FBI hounded Martin Luther King, Jr., relentlessly trying to paint him as a Communist, they were simply carrying on the thirty-year history of the service. Congress shut down FDR's Federal Theater Project in the 1930s because it gave blacks and whites the opportunity to act together on stage—a clear sign of Communism to Congressman Dies.

Hammett was active in many writers organizations, and in many organizations devoted to racial justice and civil rights. A few years after leaving prison, Hammett was back in front of Congress, this time before Joe McCarthy's committee. The Senator believed Hammett could only have named his first novel *Red Harvest* because he was a Red himself.

While it's true that in the thirties and forties Hammett openly supported the Communist Party, Blanche Knopf actually named *Red Harvest*—she thought Hammett's original title of *Poisonville* would put off readers. McCarthy even went so far as to remove copies of Hammett's novels from all American embassies so that State Department employees wouldn't be exposed to his Communist writings. When Hammett died in 1961, a veteran of both World Wars as well as the McCarthy-era Blacklist, the FBI tried to stop his burial in Arlington.

Although Hammett exaggerated his role—and even

his presence—in some of the Pinkerton Agency's high-profile cases, he did have a first-hand knowledge of crime and criminals that other noir writers didn't possess. In a 1934 introduction to the *Maltese Falcon*, Hammett wrote:

> Spade had no original. He is what most private detectives I worked with would like to have been and what quite a few in their cockier moments thought they approached. For your private detective does not want to be an erudite solver of riddles in the Sherlock Holmes manner; he wants to be a hard and shifty fellow, able to take care of himself in any situation, able to get the best of anybody he comes in contact with, whether criminal, innocent bystander or client.

Somehow, in putting his private fantasy of himself onto paper, Hammett created a landscape into which each reader, from Dorothy Parker to Joe McCarthy and beyond, could project their own image.

Hammett and Carroll John Daly created raw individualists who cared for nobody. We were supposed to admire their self-sufficiency, not like them. Raymond Chandler reclothed these hard-boiled, amoral men with the trappings of the old cowboy chivalry of Natty Bumppo or the Ingalls' Mr. Edwards.

Philip Marlowe "might seduce a duchess . . . [but] he would not spoil a virgin; if he [was] a man of honor in one thing, he [was] that in all things." In *Farewell, My*

Lovely, Marlowe is tough with Velma, the ex-night-club singer who betrays her faithful lover and lands him with a murder rap. But Marlowe protects the virginal Anne Riordan, not even kissing her when she wants him to, because he doesn't want her moving into the world of the spoiled.

It is the rich and powerful, in the hard-boiled story, who cause mischief. They are the union bosses or corporate executives or doctors or lawyers who have position and prestige to hold on to. They have retreated into their own isolation, a place where they try to use money and power as a shield between themselves and the rest of the world.

This is even truer of my work than of Chandler's. In *Indemnity Only*, my first novel, which I wrote with a very conscious eye on Chandler (I had the *Lady in the Lake* open on my lap), V I Warshawski is in Chicago's ultra-wealthy North Shore suburbs, talking to the family of a slain banking executive. One of them says to her:

"Are you trying to threaten us?"

"If you mean, am I threatening to find out the truth, the answer is yes . . ."

"Just a minute, Ted," Jack said, waving an arm at the older man. "I know how to deal with her." He nodded at me. "Come on, name your price," he said, pulling out his checkbook.

My fingers itched to bring out the Smith & Wesson and pistol-whip him. "Grow up, Thorndale . . . There

are things in this life that money can't buy. Regardless
of what you, or your mother-in-law, or the mayor of
Winnetka says, I am investigating this murder—these
murders."

I laughed a little, mirthlessly. "Two days ago, John
Thayer tried to give me $5,000 to buy me out of this
case. You guys up here on the North Shore live in some
kind of dream world. You think you can buy a cover-up
for anything that goes wrong in your lives, just like you
hire the garbage men to take away your filth or [the
maid] here to clean it up and carry it outside for you. It
doesn't work that way. John Thayer is dead. He
couldn't pay enough to get whatever filth he was
involved in away from him . . ."

The self-sufficiency of the rich is more fiction than
fact. The powerful believe their position insulates them
from everything but fulfilling their own desires. It is
part of the function of the detective novel to show that
no one is so isolated—murder occurs and forces a
confrontation with the rest of society.

In a sense, the villains of the private eye novel are the
Roger Williamses of the corporate world—what they
want counts far more with them than what the good of
the community as a whole demands. And in a funny
way, the private eye, or at least *my* private eye, has
moved out of the loner Natty Bumppo tradition and
into the community.

I recently re-read Chandler's novels. The first time

through, I was struck most by his villainous vamps, but on this recent reading, Philip Marlowe's loneliness stood out. Except for an occasional chess game with someone in the police department, he is alone all the time. On the two occasions when a woman spends the night with him, he is so upset that in the morning he tears the bed apart.

My detective couldn't survive with so much loneliness. On the personal, micro level, she needs friends, dogs, lovers—she needs continuity and connection. On the larger stage, where she's working, she's actively engaged in crimes that affect whole communities.

In *Fire Sale*, the twelfth novel in the series, she gets involved in a criminal investigation as a result of volunteering to coach the girl's basketball team at her old high school. The case takes her into the filthy swamp waters of South Chicago, it takes her into the storefront churches where her girls' families seek consolation for their barren lives, it takes her into the heart of the harsh economic realities these families face, and it leads to her almost dying in the mountains of garbage the city dumps in that neighborhood.

At the end, she's made a few things right for a very few people, but she feels it's just a drop in the bucket of need on the south side. Unlike Philip Marlowe, who would sit alone, brooding with his bottle of rye, his chess board and his records, V I goes out to dinner with her oldest friend, the doctor, Lotty Herschel.

I told her how discouraged I felt. She frowned in disapproval, or disagreement.

"Victoria, you know my grandfather, my father's father, was a very observant Jew."

I nodded, surprised: she rarely talked about her dead family.

"During the terrible winter we spent together in 1938, the fifteen of us crowded into two rooms in the Vienna ghetto, he gathered all his grandchildren together and told us that the Rabbis say when you die, and present yourself before the Divine Justice, you will be asked four questions: were you fair and honest in your business dealings? Did you spend loving time with your family? Did you study Torah? And last, but important, did you live in hope for the coming of the Messiah? We were living then without food, let alone hope, but he refused to live hopelessly, my Zeyde Radbuka.

"Me, I don't believe in God, let alone the coming of the Messiah. But I did learn from my zeyde that you must live in hope, the hope that your work can make a difference in the world. Yours does, Victoria. You cannot wave a wand and clear away the rubble of the dead steel mills, or the broken lives in South Chicago. But you went back to your old home, you took three girls who never thought about the future and made them want to have a future, made them want to get a college education. You got Rose Dorrado a job so she can support her children. If a Messiah ever does

come, it will only be because of people like you, doing
these small hard jobs, making small changes in this
hard world."

It was a small comfort, and that night at dinner it felt
like a cold one. But as the grey Chicago winter lingered,
I found myself warmed by her grandfather's hope.

It's a curious transposition that I find in my work.
When I started writing, it was in conscious emulation of
the private eye myth. Marlowe lived alone? V I Warshawski lived alone. Marlowe was an orphan? I killed
V I's beloved parents with a line of writing. Marlowe
got beaten up a third of the way into the novel? A third
of the way into *Indemnity Only*, some thugs jumped
V I in her stairwell and knocked her out.

But without my planning it deliberately, a community began infiltrating my loner hero's life right from
the start. Dr. Lotty Herschel arrived first, and with her
came Lotty's friends, lovers, her clinic staff, her patients, even, in *Killing Orders*, her disreputable coun-
terfeiter uncle. V I's parents died before the beginning
of *Indemnity Only*, but they are very present in the
novels; she remembers their advice, their criticism, and
above all, their deep and abiding love for her. She
serves on the board of a women's shelter, she works
with young people, she shares two dogs with an old man
who lives in her apartment building.

It's the hyper-wealthy criminals she meets who are
the cowboys. They are not men, or even women, of

honor; they are thoroughly tainted by greed, and by a sense of entitlement to everything in the lives of the people around them, including those lives themselves.

These corporate cowboys are the descendants of Roger Williams, but they are his twisted, corrupted heirs. Williams acted out of an urgent sense of what was right, what was needful for salvation. Today's loners are ruthless, unconcerned with the eternal, their eyes fixed firmly on the bottom line. If I were John Winthrop, or Roger Williams, or Lyman Beecher, I might make a sermon out of the parallel between the bottom line and the lower depths of hell.

My detective moves back and forth between community and isolation. When she is alone, it is because she is prompted by the same impulse that led Williams to oppose the Massachusetts Bay colony: the fear that the community has been taken over by the unjust. She seeks, as Lincoln said, "firmness in the right as God gives us to see the right."

She never claims that she is infallible, that her point of view is the only one, but she will walk alone if she has to. In this, she is tied closely to the heroic cowboys, to the *Virginian*, to Shane, or even Philip Marlowe. In our nation's mythology, honorable people have to take the law into their own hands to preserve fundamental, immutable Justice. This is Justice with a capital J because justice with a small j has been bought and perverted by the powerful.

V I is not pretentious: she does not try to save the

world—she knows she cannot. But in her own small milieu, she tries, as Lincoln did, to "bind up . . . wounds, to care for him who shall have borne the battle and for his widow and his orphan."

I would give much to find a hero of that stature today. Whenever I go to Washington, I stop at the Lincoln memorial and look up at Mr. Lincoln, at his sad, wise, kind face. I pray to him to come back and save the Republic; I have learned over the years that many people do this same thing. We don't need the reckless cowboys who are galloping today across the world's range, despoiling it. But we very much need a person who is willing to be that heroic loner, to stand for Justice even as charlatans and thugs are tearing down her walls. In the absence of Lincoln, we will have to make do with our private eyes.

Notes

1 Harriet Beecher Stowe's older sister, Catherine, was engaged in the 1840s to a young man who drowned at sea. Her Congregational minister father, Lyman Beecher, told her that with no evidence to prove his saving conversion, her fiancé was damned. While Harriet wrote *Uncle Tom's Cabin*, Catherine spent years devising a theology that allowed for her fiancé's salvation.

2 In Rhode Island, Williams became close to the Narraganset tribe. While Winthrop and most Puritans believed the Indians were allies, if not incarnations, of the devil, Williams accepted their essential humanity. He translated the bible into Narraganset, devising an alphabet for the language. As he developed Rhode Island into a colony, he allowed other religions to hold services; in that way he was far more tolerant than Winthrop and the Massachusetts Bay colony.

3 The title of the lecture John Winthrop delivered on board the *Arbella* right before the Massachusetts Bay Puritans landed in present-day Salem. See Chapter 5, p. 109, for a detailed discussion of his words.

4 Chandler was actually born in Chicago in 1888, only a few miles from my own present home. His father abandoned his mother before his birth, and when he was a few months old, his mother returned to her native England, where she reared him in company with her two aunts. As a young man, Chandler was an aesthete who aspired to be a second Oscar Wilde. When the *Westminster Review* repeatedly rejected his writing, he moved to Canada. He had a checkered career, including distinguished service with a Canadian regiment in World War I, but ended up in California doing PR for the oil industry. When he lost his job, he returned to his first love, writing, but chose the mystery; he deliberately emulated Hemingway's style, to move as far as possible from the style of his early failures.

5 The Military Commissions Act signed into law in October, 2006, essentially gives the president the power to create his own ethics and law, and he is definitely not interested in the opinions of others on that subject. In the same month the United Nation's chief investigator on torture, Manfred Nowak, told a news conference that "all too frequently" governments respond to criticism about their jails and arrest policies by saying they handle detainees the same way as the United States. Jordan's government told Nowak its detainee policy "can't be wrong if it is also done by the United States." From the *LA Times*, October 24, 2006.

5

Truth, Lies, and Duct Tape

Several years ago, I had the privilege of being a Visiting Scholar at Wolfson College, Oxford. All my ideas of Oxford were taken from the crime novels of Dorothy Sayers and Michael Innes. I saw myself punting on the Cherwell, snoozing, like Harriet Vane, in the arms of Duke Humfrey—the Oxford nickname for the original fifteenth-century part of the Bodleian Library—and returning to a cozy bed-sitting room, where I hosted little sherry parties while admiring beautiful vistas of college gardens through Elizabethan windows.

The reality was a bit different. True, the Bodleian awed me with its history, its old winding staircases, and its card catalog, written by hand in outsize volumes. The rest of my fantasy remained just that, a fantasy. It was too cold and rainy during my eleven-week tenure to punt. And the college housed me in a building which had been a nursing home until the Oxford County Council condemned it, whereupon Wolfson bought it to serve as housing for graduate students and visiting scholars. My room was on the ground floor. I shared the third-floor bathroom with five male students whose many gifts did not include personal hygiene.

After a while I began to feel like a caricature of Katharine Hepburn in the *African Queen*. I carried Dettol—a British equivalent of Clorox spray—with me to the bathroom at all times. When I showered, I encased myself in plastic, quickly sticking an arm or leg under the water, always wearing plastic slippers— which I sprayed with Dettol once I was back in my own room.

V I Warshawski, my fictional detective, has, at her best, haphazard ideas of housekeeping. These so exactly mirror my own that when my former Swedish publisher asked me why she was so messy—and I said I wrote what I knew—he backed away in disgust. This may, indeed, be why he stopped publishing me. Under these circumstances, people may not want to imagine the condition of a bathroom that made me wrap myself in plastic and Dettol.

Lately, whenever I fly, that nursing home/dormitory comes vividly to mind. Everyone knows the routine: we take off our shoes and walk in our stockings, or even bare feet, across a filthy floor. We must place not only our overcoats, but also our suit jackets in a tub that has held other people's shoes. On one trip, when I was pulled over for extra screening, I watched, helpless, as the security staff stuck bins and shoes on top of my velvet blazer and my hat. When I protested, they naturally prolonged my time in the penalty box. I wait for the day when I develop athlete's foot in my scalp.

*   *   *

Dirty flying feels symptomatic of our life nowadays. It's as though the debris of the World Trade Center has coated our minds and hands as well as the floors of the airports we walk through. Every aspect of life in contemporary America is affected by the public reaction to the events of September 11: a ruinous war in Iraq, the threat, as I write this in the fall of 2006, that the United States will compound the sins we committed in attacking Iraq by going to war against Iran; the erosion of our civil liberties; the collapse of our economy, so that we cannot afford to fund programs for the public good, even if the government had the will to do so; and over it all, the use of language to distort, to corrupt, to lie, on a scale only George Orwell or Joseph Goebbels might have imagined.

During this time, Americans have been angry and confused. Our sense of self as a country has always been an optimism bordering on arrogance, dating to before we were a country. When John Winthrop was leading his group of Puritans from England to Massachusetts Bay in 1630, he lectured them that:

> [W]e must consider that we shall be as a city upon a hill, the eyes of all people are upon us; so that if we shall deal falsely with our god in this work we have undertaken and so cause him to withdraw his present help from us, we shall be made a story and a byword through the world.

This sense of being set apart from other people, of being better, more holy, more surely right, has persisted through the four centuries of European life in America. This sense has meant different things to different people. To some, it has meant a freedom to experiment, to try new things, not to be bound by shibboleths. Others took it to mean that our soldiers and military were invincible. They can't figure out why the country that twice saved Europe in the twentieth century, landing in France in 1917 with the cry, "Lafayette, we are here!" can't dominate Iraq, Afghanistan, indeed, the whole world, with our military might.

To others, our commitment to justice and the rule of law, even in the shameful days of segregation and lynch mobs, did, indeed, make us a city upon a hill, a beacon for all oppressed people everywhere.

I myself grew up in the belief that America was a haven. The Statue of Liberty, "the Mother of Exiles," welcomed my twelve-year-old grandmother when she had to flee a pogrom and sailed, alone, into New York Harbor in 1911. I knew as a child my own existence was only possible because America had welcomed my granny, or, at least, not turned its back on her (as happened to Jewish children 25 years later, when America denied them entry visas on the brink of the Nazi invasion of Poland).

I also grew up when the Federal Government sent marshals to protect black children as they had to walk to school past angry, rock-throwing mobs of white adults. I grew up when the Supreme Court struck down laws that permitted discrimination in schools, the workplace, in the bedroom, indeed, in the courts themselves.

I cannot find words to express the depth of my loss, or my outrage, to see my country abrogate treaties abroad, and violate the very heart and bones of our Constitution here at home. Some of us feel corrupt and tainted, others weak and angry, and the mood of the country is ugly. As a writer, in a time like this, it is hard to know what to say and how to say it.

The master of words put it this way:

> This land of such dear souls, this dear dear land,
> Dear for her reputation through the world,
> Is now leas'd out—I die pronouncing it—
> Like to a tenement or pelting farm.
> England, bound in with the triumphant sea,
> Whose rocky shore beats back the envious siege
> Of wat'ry Neptune, is now bound in with shame,
> With inky blots and rotten parchment bonds;
> That England, that was wont to conquer others,
> Hath made a shameful conquest of itself.[1]

Every writer's difficult journey is a movement from silence to speech. We must be intensely private and interior in order to find a voice and a vision—and we must bring our work to an outside world where the market, or public outrage, or even government censorship can destroy our voice.

This is not a new problem in America. When Melville published *Moby Dick* in 1851, the reception by both public and critics was extremely hostile. The book we today consider a high achievement of American letters sold a handful of copies, about 500 in Melville's lifetime. The reception left Melville confused—and poor. He worked at dead-end jobs to support his family, and struggled at night to write. For almost thirty years he produced only fragments, wisps of prose that he burned with the dawn. At one point he wrote to Hawthorne:

> I am so pulled hither and thither by circumstances. The coolness, the silent grass-growing mood in which a [person] ought to compose—that can seldom be mine. Dollars damn me, and the malicious Devil is forever grinning in upon me . . . What I feel most moved to write, that is banned [by the market] because it will not pay.

Kate Chopin, a single mother who supported six children with her writing during the 1880s and '90s, received such a storm of criticism for her novel *The Awakening* that Scribner's actually halted publication of her next book, which was on the printing presses at the time. The story of a woman's attempt to liberate herself from a stifling marriage by having an affair was too much for the 300 critics who panned *The Awakening* in 1899. Chopin herself died five years later, at the age of fifty-four, without seeing her work come back into print.

Silence does not mean consent. Silence means death. When we have something to say and we are afraid to speak, or forbidden to speak, we feel as though we've been walled into a closet. Silence can come from the market, as it did for Melville. It can come from public hysteria, as it did for Kate Chopin. It can come from the government as outright censorship. Today in America we are finding pressure to silence coming from all three sources.

1. The changed marketplace

The writer Calvin Trillen once commented that, "The shelf life of a modern hardback writer is somewhere between the milk and the yogurt." If you want to know why that's the case, turn to that astute social commentator Sylvester Stallone: "Yo," he said, "I'm astounded by people who take eighteen years to write something. That's how long it took that guy to write *Madame Bovary*, and was it ever on the bestseller list?"[2]

In his inimitable way, Sly spoke up for the industry. Although he often portrays the loner hero succeeding against all odds, Stallone has become one of the richest people in America by being a star, and by being bank-rolled by the conglomerates he fights on-screen. (I should note in the interest of accuracy that Sly was a little off—it actually only took Flaubert five years to write *Madame Bovary*. Still quite a difference from the three days Stallone says it took him to create the script for *Rocky*.)

I published my first novel some twenty years ago. It took my agent a year to find a publisher willing to take a chance on a female private eye in America's heartland, but he kept on plugging because there were more than forty publishers to go to. They had names to conjure with: Alfred A. Knopf, Charles Scribner, G. B. Putnam. When you said those names you thought of books. You thought of Wharton or Hammett or Faulkner.

Today there are essentially seven publishers. And their names include Gulf & Western, Disney, Time-Warner. You say those names and you think of— Mickey Mouse. It's taking the guy eighteen years— or even five–to write about a provincial doctor's wife? Dump the jerk. Which is exactly what Harper-Collins (part of the Murdoch empire) did a few years ago— canceled contracts with a hundred writers as easily as you might cancel a magazine subscription.

As media multi-nationals bought up publishing houses by the cord, they took management away from book people and put it in the hands of marketing and accounting MBAs. Today's editors spend more time reading profit-and-loss statements and running marketing scenarios through Excel and PowerPoint than they do reading manuscripts. Simon & Schuster has been the industry leader in turning books into products. Early in their conglomerate life, they brought in the head of Procter and Gamble's Pampers division, who announced that a book was a product like a Pamper and could be marketed accordingly.

Of course, publishers and booksellers alike have always published and sold books to make money, but there can't be another product in the marketplace where so many people historically came to it out of a deep love for the product itself: the product—what a name to use for the written word that can breathe life into the soul.

While the Knopfs or Bennet Cerf would look at their whole list to make up a profit-and-loss statement, the Procter and Gamble approach meant that each book became a profit center. Bennet Cerf would publish a writer like Faulkner because he believed in his work, even though *Absalom, Absalom!* or *The Sound and the Fury* barely broke even. Cerf did this because he looked at the profitability of his whole list, rather than expecting each title to be a bestseller. Faulkner sold very few books before being anointed with Swedish holy water. Today he probably wouldn't stay in print long enough for the Nobel committee to discover him.

In the eighties, at the same time that publishing was contracting, distribution outlets were consolidating. Distribution outlets used to be called bookstores. But bookstores are not where most people buy books these days. According to the *New Yorker*, over half US book sales take place in price clubs, where books and toilet paper are viewed simply as different forms of trees. Another quarter are sold in the mega-chains like Barnes & Noble or Borders. Eight percent are sold on-line or in airports or supermarkets, and the remainder in what dinosaurs like me think of as bookstores.

The consolidation of publishers into a handful of media conglomerates and the emergence of the chains and price clubs as the big players in book sales came hand in hand with the creation of the star system for writers.

A star is basically a brand. A brand is a writer, or—as the president of Simon & Schuster called us a few years ago—a content provider, whose name on the package guarantees a sale. Harrison Ford or Julia Roberts bring you into the theater regardless of the nature or quality of the movie they're in. Grisham or Cornwell on the jacket gets you to buy the package—I mean book— regardless of the nature or quality of its content. Or, in the case of Clancy or Patterson, regardless of whether the person named on the jacket has actually provided the content.

If you're a bookstore stocking brands, you don't have to have a staff who reads or knows books in order to sell them. You only need a high school student who can operate a cash register. And while the megastores do carry a gazillion titles, they actually have decreased book sales over the last decade, by about ten percent a year. Almost half of megastore sales each year are of 500 different titles out of the 150,000 that they stock. Twenty percent of their sales are of the top hundred sellers they carry.

All of this has dire consequences for diversity in what

is published. Kate Chopin was by no means the last established writer to find herself without a publisher in America; their numbers have been growing rapidly. Writers of longstanding, with ten or even twenty published novels to their names, with sales that made a profit for their companies, can't find a publisher today.

Concentration in any industry basically benefits one group and one group only: the majority shareholders. It doesn't help consumers, as anyone looking for health care, or paying a heating bill knows. Right now, you can buy a bestselling book for less in a chain or a price club than in a bookstore, but your choice of books is diminishing.

Because they are such big players in the business, big box retailers help make publishing decisions. Their buyers have a say in everything from jacket design to what books get published, or published in a big way. Their goal is to find titles that will turn over effortlessly. You don't need a literate staff to sell peanut butter, and you don't need a literate staff to sell the "branded" books that sit in the bins next to the peanut bar jars and panty-hose eggs. In a meeting with Random House executives, Costco stressed that they will replace books with dog food if the dog food is selling better.

Forces of silence can come more subtly from the market than from the edicts of a totalitarian state. In a country where TV and newspapers shed their reporters to maximize profits for a handful of investors, it becomes harder all the time to find reliable information. Instead, we are treated to innuendos, glib one-liners, and outright lies—the biggest, of course, being that we could prove Saddam Hussein caused the 9/11 attacks, and prove that he had massive nuclear and biological weapons. Time and again in the last five years, the government has been caught paying media to run puff pieces about its policies. Armstrong Williams, a columnist syndicated by Tribune Media Services, one of America's largest media holding companies, was paid $240,000 to promote Bush's "No Child Left Behind" act; the Tribune let him go only after *USA Today* discovered the payments. Williams was then hired by the right-wing Heritage Foundation's website to write a column for them, in which he used the administration's trumped-up numbers to attack Social Security.

In March, 2005, the *New York Times* reported that more than twenty federal agencies, including the State and Defense Departments, create fake news clips, including actors who pose as reporters, conducting staged interviews with administration mouthpieces—at a cost to taxpayers of around $254 million.[3] These and other reports have not stopped the administration from also trying to open an office of "disinformation" under different names. All these acts make it ever harder to tell truth from lies.

Fiction can provide a form of truth: not the truth of hard news carefully investigated, but that of real emotions, carefully explored. But when the same media giants who own our TV stations and newspapers also own our book publisher, then it's time to worry about what voices we will be allowed to hear—whose truth, what truth will fall to the maximized bottom line. Those books that stir our souls, those books that come from Melville's silent, grass-growing mood, will not survive in a world that exists only by the narrow criterion of that line. We have become, as Melville said, damned by dollars.

2. Libraries and civil liberties

When I was starting out as a writer, libraries played an enormous role in my success. My first book, *Indemnity Only*, sold about 3,500 copies; 2,500 of those were to libraries. Today's publishers expect a novel to sell about 25,000 hardcover copies before they will keep on a writer, but twenty-plus years ago, one-seventh that number was considered a modest success, and my (now defunct) publisher requested a second novel.

Everything is harder for new writers now, in many ways, and one of those ways is the steep drop in book sales to libraries. Somehow in the last two decades, Americans have decided that it is outrageous to pay taxes to support the common good. As a result, we have repeatedly cut library budgets, until today libraries have about a third of the money to buy books that they did twenty years ago.

Of course, a lot of people resent paying taxes for anything that supports the public good, whether for libraries, schools, or health care. This is a debate we've been having in America for 150 years—public libraries and public schools were called socialist or communist by many in the Victorian-era anti-tax movement. Similar people are making similar arguments today, and, along with schools and health care, libraries are suffering.

Just as libraries have been heavy losers in contemporary budget wars, they have also been on the front lines of today's assaults against America's most cherished liberties. This assault began with, but isn't limited to, the USA Patriot Act, passed in the feverish fearful weeks immediately after 9/11. The fact that then Attorney-General John Ashcroft (known in Missouri as "the Crisco Kid" because he supposedly anoints himself with oil every time he receives an important promotion[4]) had a 300-page bill ready for Congress within two weeks of the attacks, suggests to that he had the legislation prepared long in advance of them: from the start of its reign, the Bush White House has been obsessed with secrecy and executive privilege.

Whatever the background of the Patriot Act, it was passed without debate, and with only one dissenting vote in the US Senate. Many members of Congress confessed that they hadn't even read the Act before voting on it. In the five years since its passage, although the Justice Department has often claimed the Act has helped thwart terrorism, they have not yet come up with any actual examples. The Act has, however, given the FBI, the new Department of Homeland Security, and local law enforcement an amazing and terrifying arsenal of weapons against citizens and ordinary criminals.

About a decade ago, I was on the fringe of an exciting Chicago drama. What happened was this: a couple of men—call them Ben and Jerry—owned a business together on the city's north side. They had a standard insurance policy for a partnership, so that if one partner died insurance would cover the loss of his investment in the firm.

Ben was having an affair with Jerry's wife, Lucy, when Ben got greedy: he wanted Lucy and the whole business all to himself. Lucy agreed, and she helped Ben find a hitman to kill her husband. Once Jerry was dead they could collect the insurance and live agreeably, if not happily, ever after. Lucy found a real hitman, not an off-duty cop. (I'm forever reading about unfortunate women who go into bars looking for hitmen to kill their husbands, only to find that they've hooked up with an off-duty police officer, who arrests them. It seems like our police could have better things to do with their time than hang out in bars misleading trusting women, but that's another story. Our story is about Ben and Lucy and their real hitman.)

At the eleventh hour, Lucy got cold feet and ratted to

the cops, who stopped the hitman right before he killed
Jerry. Ben was arrested, and ultimately found guilty of
conspiring to commit murder. When the cops arrested
the hitman, they found a stack of index cards next to
him on the car seat. The top card read, "*Killing Orders*
—Sara Paretsky."

The cops were excited; they thought they'd found the
mastermind behind the hit. At two a.m., they raced off
to the state's attorney to apply for an emergency
warrant. Fortunately for me, the assistant state's attorney catching night duty was a mystery reader. He
explained that *Killing Orders* was the title of one of
my novels. The hitman had a list of books that he
wanted to read while he hid out after the job—I guess I
should feel flattered that mine made the top of his list.
The cops never did arrest me.

Nowadays, that story has the potential to play out
differently. Under the Patriot Act, the police would not
have to explain why they wanted a warrant—they could
claim that they thought my work was related to a
criminal investigation with a *possible* connection to
terror without saying one word more to the state's
attorney. To get a warrant they don't have to show
probable cause: they do not have to offer proof of any
kind. They could take me away and make me account
for myself without allowing me to talk to a lawyer. They
could hold me indefinitely without charging me. They
could keep me from telling my family where I was.

They can tap my phone. They no longer need a

warrant for this wiretap. Even if they never arrested me, agents could come into my house, search and seize my files, my books, and download data from my computer, without showing me a warrant, or indeed, telling me that they had been in my house, if they came when I wasn't at home.

A Buffalo, New York artist found this out in 2004, to his sorrow and astonishment. Steve Kurtz was creating a piece for an exhibition on genetically modified food, and had ordered non-toxic bacteria from a lab that routinely supplies such organisms to high school and college science classes. When his wife suddenly died that May, and Kurtz called 911, the FBI arrived ahead of the EMT crew—they had been tapping his phone and his e-mail without a warrant or probable cause.

The FBI, in concert with the Buffalo police, arrested him, they held him without charging him, they seized all his books, his hard drive and his papers. When the autopsy proved his wife had died of a heart attack in her sleep, they finally let him go home, but for two years, he has faced trial on unspecified charges. In a reprise of Kafka, the government, unable to decide on a charge, has kept changing the trial date.

A particularly nasty feature of the case is the government claim to a judge that they had found documents proving Kurtz supported terrorism. At one court hearing, they produced their sole evidence: a postcard announcing a museum exhibition that was illustrated with a photograph of an exploded car with Arabic writing next to it.[5] The judge was furious when the government finally had to produce their evidence in court—he had not been allowed to see it when he issued them their search warrant.

The government is still considering charging Kurtz with mail and wire fraud; penalties for both were greatly increased under the Patriot Act. In the meantime, Kurtz's travel is restricted, and he is subject to frequent random drug tests. The man who supplied him with the bacteria, who has also been the target of federal investigations, suffered two major strokes as a result of the stress of being under constant investigation without being charged or tried.

Kurtz's situation may be extreme, but it is not illegal, nor even unusual. The law can seize books, papers, hard drives of any individual in this country. They can seize them from your library or your bookstore.

In addition to the powers of the Patriot Act, the government has been using National Security Agency letters in a massive way. Since passage of the Patriot Act, the FBI has issued 30,000 national security letters a year. Before the Patriot Act, they issued 300 such letters a year. These letters compel libraries, bookstores, or any business, such as a hotel, to give up all records about its customers or its guests to the NSA.

NSA letters allow the FBI to follow not only the e-mails and phone calls of the target of the national security letter, but of any person the target is in touch with. For instance, if my local bookstore received such a letter, they would have to turn over all their customer records to the feds, who could then, without telling me, go into my computer and get the e-mails of everyone I ever correspond with, and go into *their* e-mails.

This actually happened in Las Vegas in 2003. All the hotels in the city were compelled to turn over their guest lists, including credit card, e-mail, and other information. The only reason this came to light was that casinos balked at supplying the data and tried to protest it: the city's motto is, "What happens in Vegas, stays in Vegas."

A further feature of both the Patriot Act and NSA letters is a gag law. Recipients of letters or of Patriot Act subpoenas are forbidden, under penalty of five years imprisonment, to reveal that they received letters or subpoenas.

Librarians have had one tiny victory in this scenario: a Connecticut librarian was arrested in 2005 for telling a lawyer that he had received a National Security letter demanding access to his library's records. In April, 2006, courts ruled that he could reveal the fact that he had received the letter to his lawyer. So far, the courts have upheld a DOJ gag order that keeps the public from knowing the librarian's name, and the ruling doesn't affect the FBI's demand for his library's records (although his name and that of three other targeted librarians have seeped into the press).

Armed with a National Security letter, the government could obtain the records of bookstores and find

out everyone buying my book. As a deputy attorney-
general told Congress, "Libraries and book[stores]
should not become safe havens for terrorists."

Every state in the union has laws, either written or
established by legal precedent, to protect the privacy of
library patrons: what we read, what we check out, what
we look at on-line, is our business—even if we're
reading *Killing Orders*.

The Patriot Act overturns those confidentiality laws.
The Patriot Act allows the government to compel
libraries to produce circulation records, Internet-use
records, or information stored in any medium. If served
with a subpoena, libraries and librarians may not
disclose the existence of the subpoena, nor the fact
that records were produced as a result of it. Patrons
cannot be told that their records were given to the FBI,
nor that they are the subject of an FBI investigation. In
addition, the government does not have to demonstrate
"probable cause" to get a subpoena issued. Instead, the
law enforcement agent only needs to claim that records
may be related to an ongoing investigation involving
terrorism or intelligence activities. The law that set up
the Department of Homeland Security further did away
with checks on the government's authority to seize
records and conduct wiretaps.

According to a survey conducted by the Library
Research Center at the University of Illinois in 2002,
our government has seized circulation and Internet-use
records from at least eleven percent and perhaps as

many as thirty percent of the nation's libraries since passage of the Patriot Act.[6] We don't know which libraries were involved, because if librarians report that their library has been involved in a search of records, they face arrest and imprisonment.

I wrote the Library Research Center recently to see if they were updating their survey to include 2003–05 data, and learned that the FBI denounced the study's author in the pages of the *Wall Street Journal* as a supporter of terrorism; she has been threatened with unspecified reprisals if she continues the study.

That news made me sick.

We like to think in America that we are all four-square for individualism and for individual expression, and that only in totalitarian states do people cave in to threats. I'm not so hopeful. Perhaps this is because I grew up in an idyllic Midwestern town in the 1950s, when America was obsessed with the threat of Communism.

In Lawrence, Kansas, people felt the Cold War as something real and very close. Protecting Lawrence, and America, against Communism was a local obsession. A high school teacher working on a PhD in Soviet history was forced to resign, since only a Communist would want to learn Russian. The daily newspaper was vigilant in pointing out godless elements in town and inciting mob action against them. When my parents protested a religious revival held in the town high school—at which student attendance was mandatory—the paper printed their names and phone number and urged citizens to call to tell them how little use America had for Communist-loving atheists. For weeks my parents got hate calls in the middle of the night urging them to go back where they came from—southern Illinois for my mother, Brooklyn for my father.

Today, we are once more allowing panic-peddling and fear to rule us. Among many recent acts, we Americans have done the following, either directly ourselves or through our state, local, or federal governments:

Arrested a library patron in Morristown, NJ for looking at foreign-language pages on the Web. We held him for three days without charging him, without letting him call a lawyer, or notify his wife.

Arrested a man at St. Johns College in Santa Fe, New Mexico, for making a negative comment about George Bush in a chat room from the college library. We put a gag order on all the students and faculty, forbidding them to reveal that this arrest had taken place; the staff member who told me about it could be imprisoned for doing so.

Pressured a North Carolina Public Radio Station to drop a long-time sponsorship from a reproductive rights group, claiming that the Federal Communications Commission holds reproductive-rights advocates to be political groups and therefore not permissible donors to a radio station that gets some federal funding.

Interrogated a California telephone repairman for criticizing George Bush; when the man said he thought there was freedom of speech in America, the FBI said there was, but they were still writing him up.

Harassed an Iowa farmer for protesting the war by flying the American flag upside-down and backwards.

Imprisoned Georgia novelist Joshilynn Jackson for discrepancies between her driver's license (issued in her married name) and social security card (issued in her birth name). Embarrassed local police explained that federal anti-terrorism laws gave them no leeway in such situations.

Assaulted French foreign exchange students because their government opposed our invasion of Iraq.

Imprisoned an eighty-one-year-old Haitian Baptist minister when he landed at Miami airport on October 29, 2004 traveling with a valid passport and visa. We took away his blood pressure medicine and ridiculed him for not speaking clearly through his voice-box. He collapsed and died in our custody five days later.

Held people without charging them for over four years; many, still in prison, face indefinite incarceration.

Issued death threats on right-wing radio shows against New York and Los Angeles *Times* editors and writers for revealing warrantless NSA wiretaps on tens of millions of American citizens.

Seized an innocent Canadian citizen as he changed planes at JFK, whisked him by private jet to Jordan and then handed him over to Syria for ten months of torture and interrogation. The Syrians released him after they could find no links to terrorism and a Canadian commission completely cleared his name, but the US refused to apologize and rejected a lawsuit for damages on the grounds that we would have to discuss our policies of rendition and kidnapping in court, thus revealing state secrets.

Voted, in 2006, to define the rules of the Geneva convention as we see fit, without expressly relinquishing our right to incarcerate people without charging them or trying them, to transport them to distant prisons, or to torture them—in short, giving our government, more specifically the president, power to commit acts of "Cruelty & perfidy scarcely paralleled in the most barbarous ages and totally unworthy of the Head of a civilized nation," as Thomas Jefferson put it.

I could include many other examples, but I can't bear to go on with this section.

3. Truth, Lies, and Duct-Tape

What is the appropriate response of a writer in times like these? At the most basic level, it's my job to continue to write stories that—I hope—people will want to read. More fundamentally, I think it's my job to try to fumble my way as close as I can to the truth, not to accept a slippery slipshod misuse of language or ideas, not to let the fear of arrest or public outrage lead me into self-censorship.

This particular essay began as a talk I gave to a number of libraries and state library associations about the Patriot Act and the library. I was scheduled to speak at the Toledo, Ohio public library the night before we shocked and awed Iraq. The library asked me not to deliver this talk, because it was so controversial that people were turning in their tickets rather than listen to me; the library asked me to emulate other writers in giving humorous anecdotes about my writing life (the time I was arrested for having mismatched social security and driver's license names, and other light-hearted memoirs of the post-terrorism age).

I don't like hostility. I don't relish confrontation. My upbringing has made me particularly vulnerable to angry criticism, to the implied fear of being a bad daughter, not submissive enough. I thought about acquiescing. I thought about all the times I had caved in to the demands of an angry person, and how filled with self-loathing I've been afterwards. I gave this talk, but my knees were shaking so badly I had to grip the podium throughout.

I was fortunate that night: the 500 people in the audience who'd come out in a rainstorm to hear me gave me an ovation. Many, including several abortion-rights advocates, told me afterwards that each thought she was the only person in the community who opposed the invasion, and the sacrifice of civil liberties in the name of public safety. A man who said he was a professional mercenary, fighting for US and British corporations in

Africa, said he had come to jeer and stayed to pray, as
the old Gospel line has it.

A police officer told me, under vow of not revealing
his name, that police forces all over America now feel
empowered to disregard basic safeguards on citizens'
rights. (In the spring 2006 term, the US Supreme Court
showed he was right, by overturning 800 years of
English common law precedent that makes a person's
home an inviolable space. Speaking for the majority,
Anton Scalia said that if someone's home is invaded and
trashed in error—as happens about 200 times a year,
apparently, when the police target the wrong person—
they have the remedy of civil litigation against the
police. Please pause for a minute to imagine that
scenario.)

If the crowd had booed me from the stage in Toledo
that March night, I don't know whether I would have
found the courage to keep making these remarks. I am
as weak and as easily manipulated by angry rejection as
anyone else, and certainly more than my heroes, the
great Russian poets of the twentieth century, who
risked torture, imprisonment, and death rather than
cave into the demands of an authoritarian government.

I was just starting work on my novel, *Blacklist*, when
we suffered the terrorist attack in New York City. For
some weeks I was so frozen with shock that I couldn't
write at all. When I did start work, I unconsciously
retreated from current events. I thought of a crime
based on actions back in the McCarthy era. I had a great

deal of fun creating a Gothic subplot, with a family history going back to the 1890s. I'm infatuated with fashion, and I spent some lovely days in archives studying dress designs from the 1890s through the 1930s for the women in my Gothic family.

But as *Blacklist* began to take shape, my fears about the world around me began to seep into the story in different ways, as part of one of the subplots, and as part of some of the ways in which various law enforcement groups try to silence V I. Most readers thought these subplots, or side issues, enhanced the novel, but I have also had some very strong hate mail, accusing me of hating Jesus and hating America because I question whether the FBI should be able to come into my detective's home and take her files away ("paranoid pinko liberal trash," wrote one excited fan.)

I'm not interested in writing propaganda novels, any more than I want to read them—that is, books written only to make a point—to show that four legs are better than two, or all males are testosterone-crazed villains, or women inevitably use their bodies to make good boys do bad things. There's a reason that the writers we know from Stalin's Russia are Pasternak and Akhmatova, not Gribachev, who wrote *Spring in the Victory Collective Farm*. Pasternak may have wanted to make a point, an ardently felt point, about human freedom, about the confusion that we feel in the midst of social upheavals, and how hard it is to know how to act. But he wanted to write about human beings caught up in

events, not idealized political types—and that is my
goal as well.

At the same time, books are our guides, our supports:
they show us that we are not alone in our belief in liberty
and freedom. The Russian poet Ratushinskaya, who
spent three years in a forced labor camp for her writing,
helped keep a yearning for liberty alive in her readers in
the old Soviet Union. The only way to keep ourselves free
is to speak, not to let ourselves be silenced, either by
pernicious laws, or by mob screaming.

My own stories come to me from the events around
me, but the events around me today are defying my
ability to turn them into stories. I have often written
about corporate corruption, and the cynical indiffer-
ence of large institutions to the well-being of ordinary
citizens. But Enron and Halliburton defy even my
imagination.

My detective often turns to her friend Murray Ryer-
son, a reporter, who can publicize what's happened, and
make it hard for the criminals to hold on to their jobs,
even if they get to keep their stock portfolios. But all
over America, newspapers like Murray's have been
bought by giant media conglomerates, which cut staffs
of reporters in half, because every time they lay off a lot
of people, their stock prices jump. So papers don't have
resources to investigate corporate or government scan-
dals. And many times, the newspaper or TV station is
itself part of a conglomerate that is either actively
participating in similar crimes, or won't reveal crimes

by government officials because the conglomerate wants political favors.

Whenever I sit down to write, I feel like a toy ballerina on a magnet, being twirled in circles so fast that I can't figure out what to look at. The toxicity I encounter at airports pervades the landscape these days. I feel that I'm walking under a toxic cloud, not of germs or radiation, that plastic and Dettol might keep out, but of lies. When the government tells me there's a code orange alert, to wrap myself in duct tape and plastic, but go shopping—as long as I don't buy anything French—because it's my patriotic duty to buy and run up my debt but I mustn't have bankruptcy protection, I become just about speechless from the disconnect between truth, lies—and well, duct tape.

When the government says, we will fight AIDS in Africa, but says no one can distribute or even mention condoms, I know I'm in the world of 1984.

When the president of the United States vetoes a bill allowing researchers to use embryonic stem cells and does everything he can to outlaw abortion and birth control, because he embraces a culture of life, all the while he sanctions the use of torture by his government, and oversees the daily deaths of many scores of men, women and children in the Middle East, and while he also denies money for health care to veterans and homeless children, I guess I know I'm in the modern world.

After the shameful reports out of Abu Ghraib became public knowledge, the president's chief cheerlea-

ders on AM talk radio dismissed them as no worse than
fraternity hazing. Perhaps Rush Limbaugh was right:
when George Bush was a student at Yale, he used to
enjoy branding fraternity pledges with red-hot coat-
hangers. Perhaps Abu Ghraib and Bagwam remind him
of his college days.

I hate feeling powerless. I hate my detective to be
powerless. But I can't have her act like a Robert
Ludlum super-hero, forcing the FBI and Disney to
their knees—as much as I'd like to—and walking off
unharmed, because my stories rely too much on the
world of the real. My heroes have to take their lumps
the way we all do in the world of the real. I just won't
subject V I to the ultimate lumps that some heroes have
to take. She won't die for her beliefs, she won't be
silenced, she won't sell out her friends. That is the best
I can offer her and my readers in the world of today.

I want to walk away, no, run away from all these
horrors. I want to play with words and dazzle readers
with my brilliant turns of phrase, but the times weigh
me down. Instead, I keep thinking of Anna Akhmatova,
outside the prison in Leningrad where her son was
being held by Stalin.

She wrote:

In the terrible years of the Yeshov terror, I spent
seventeen months in the prison lines of Leningrad.
Once, someone recognized me. Then a woman with

bluish lips standing behind me . . . woke up from the stupor to which everyone had succumbed and whispered in my ear (everyone spoke in whispers there):

"Can you describe this?"

And I answered: "Yes, I can."

Then something that looked like a smile passed over what had once been her face.

I can't stand idly by while my beloved country reduces its citizens to speaking in whispers out of fear of what their invisible, invasive government may do.

Because my own great comfort comes from other writers' words, my hope is that my stories may also bring readers some solace in the night, provide some lamplight on a darkened path. Twenty six hundred years ago, the poet Sappho—who saw the goddess descend from the heavens in a chariot pulled by sparrows—wrote,

> Although they are
> Only breath, words
> Which I command
> Are immortal.

As a child, in the world of books and daydreams where I sought refuge from an unfriendly world, I longed for magic, longed for the passage to Narnia or other fairylands. As an adult, I watch the sparrows outside my window closely: I still yearn enough for magic to hope they'll bring me the goddess, but ultimately I have to realize that these are hard-scrabbling urban birds, trying to stay alive in a world that's rough on small creatures, and on poets.

When I enter a library, when I enter the world of books, I feel the ghosts of the past on my shoulders, urging me to courage. I hear Patrick Henry cry to the Burgesses, "Is Life so dear, or Peace so sweet, to be purchased at the price of chains and slavery?" I hear Sojourner Truth tell me that the hand that rocks the cradle can also rock the boat, and the great abolitionist William Lloyd Garrison say, "I am in earnest, I will not be silenced."

It is my only hope, that against those forces which seek to silence us, to rob us of our voices and our precious freedoms, that my words, Sappho's words, indeed, our Constitution's words, that all these words, which are only breath, will not only endure, but triumph.

Notes

1 *Richard II*, Act II, Scene i.
2 Quoted from a *New York Times* interview on IMDb.com ,*inter alia*.
3 "And now, the Counterfeit News," *New York Times*, March 16, 2005.
4 *San Francisco Chronicle*, August 4, 2002, *inter alia*.
5 *Info Exchange*, May 19, 2005, *inter alia*.
6 The University of Illinois Library Research Center conducted this survey, which is reported on the American Library Association website. The figures have not been updated since 2002, so they are probably considerably higher.